FACING ADULT PROBLEMS
IN CHRISTIAN EDUCATION

FACING
ADULT PROBLEMS
IN
CHRISTIAN EDUCATION

By Helen Khoobyar

THE WESTMINSTER PRESS

Philadelphia

In Memory
of
My Father
who led me to the source
of
his abiding faith

CONTENTS

FACING ADULT PROBLEMS
IN CHRISTIAN EDUCATION

INTRODUCTION

There are many ways by which the subject of this book may be approached. We may engage in the history of Christian adult education; we may concern ourselves with how to organize adult study groups in a local church and suggest methods of teaching; we may make an appraisal of current interest and practice of the educational function of the church and visualize an emerging Christian adult education movement. All of these are important and even necessary if we are to know what it is that we are talking about. But much has been written in recent years that has made valuable contributions to the field. This author is grateful for the challenge presented in *A Hard Look at Adult Christian Education,* by John R. Fry, and would commend it to the attention of those who are engaged in the ministry of the church.

In spite of the current interest in Christian adult education and the rising criticism of its content and practices, the question of why adults attend classes and what actually happens to them is an exceedingly important one. It is difficult to draw the line of demarcation between Christian educators who tend to emphasize what Christian adult education *ought* to be and what is actually happening in study groups. Therefore, when we deal with this matter, we need firsthand information.

This book is the product of the author's own experience with some five thousand adults over a period of six years. The substance of the material is based on what actually happened in groups of various denominations in the states of Connecticut, Massachusetts, Rhode Island, New York, and California. The excerpts, quotations, and illustrations that appear in the book are edited from tape recordings and the notes of observers, and are offered to bring some of the major issues to the attention of the reader.

The book is mainly an attempt to describe why adults attend classes, what kind of questions they ask, and what obstacles they encounter in their Christian faith. Chapter IV discusses the purpose of Christian adult education, and the last chapter offers some thoughts for the Christian education of adults in a local church.

It is obvious that such an attempt has many limitations. First, there is always the problem of oversimplification. Within the scope of this book, all the detailed problems cannot be reported and treated adequately; therefore, a sketchy discussion such as this is apt to omit a multitude of questions and problems. Secondly, no absolute claim to objective analysis of the problems and needs of adults can be made by the author. Some subjectivity is no doubt inevitable. But the book is presented with the hope that these explorations will stimulate the reader to project fresh and bold ideas that can raise adult Christian education into concerted and adventurous enterprise, and further, encourage him to translate the implications of such vision into terms of a farsighted and practical imperative.

WHY ADULTS ATTEND STUDY GROUPS

What is the present situation with regard to Christian adult education in the church? We are told by the National Council of Churches that more than fifteen million men and women attend study groups in the U.S.A. Additional millions are involved in activities such as teaching in the church school, youth work, women's organizations, committee work, etc., which have direct educational possibilities. This is the

largest group of adults to be brought together by any institu-
tion for the purpose of study.

In addition to study groups in local churches, there are
recognized lay study centers established at Parishfield, Mich-
igan, the Faith and Life Community located at Austin,
Texas, and the Laymen's School of Religion in Berkeley,
California. All these schools represent a concern of the whole
church for an understanding of the Christian faith and for
Christian witness in the world. But before we stop on this
encouraging note, let us also add a sobering one: in spite of
numbers and enthusiasm, generally speaking only a fragment
of the total adult constituency of the church is involved in
some serious study. The rest of the adults are either indifferent or have no opportunity for Christian education.

What are the reasons for this upsurge of interest in adult
education? One very simple reason may be that it is fashion-
able to attend study groups. It is the thing to do. It has almost become a fad and an end in itself. Some believe that
often a collection of religiously inclined individuals come together for fellowship and sociability; sometimes a group of
like-minded people are drawn together by sympathetic asso-
ciations and congenial interest in the nurture of their spiritual life.

All these reasons may or may not be true. We would like,
however, to focus our attention less upon generalizations
than upon more specific questions, namely: Who are these
adults who participate in study groups? and What are their
real reasons (perhaps unconscious) for being in the group?
Without our trying to guess their unconfessed, mixed motives, we shall give an answer based on what adults themselves have expressed.

The adult constituency of the church has never been more
ready to learn. The majority of adults who attend study
groups honestly admit and openly recognize that their knowledge of the Bible and of the Christian faith is almost nil;

that their comprehension of worship and the sacraments is vague and confused; that their participation in the world as Christians is superficial. They realize that instead of retreating in confusion and uncertainty, it is time to " do something about it." On the other hand, there are those who have some vague ideas about God, sin, Christ, and the church. They do not understand the full implications of these words, nor are they able to articulate their beliefs, but they regard them as significant and meaningful and are eager to do further study and thinking.

On the whole, there is much confusion in adults' understanding of almost all the doctrines of the Christian faith. Many of these problems stem from both misunderstanding and too literal understanding of the Christian faith and its concepts.

The layman's version of Kierkegaard's famous phrase, " How to become a Christian? " is, " How can I be a real Christian? " There is the obvious evidence of a quest for a living faith and a mature and sincere search on the part of many people for honest answers to complex and difficult problems of life. They consider the Christian faith to be of utmost importance but seriously doubt that their being Christian distinguishes them in any significant way from " non-Christians." " Does being a member of the church make any difference? " " Because a person is a Christian, is he in better relationship with others than one who is not? " Some are even doubtful whether being a Christian really makes any difference in their own lives. " Does being a disciple of Christ today offer any answers to life's problems? " Those who are aware of their responsibility as Christians are disturbed by their inability to witness to their faith. " I have a neighbor who is not a believer. When we get together she asks me all kinds of religious questions. But how can I help her when I don't know myself? I want to learn what my faith is all about! "

Parents who admit their religious inarticulateness and

theological and Biblical illiteracy are anxious to know how to answer Johnny's questions: " Who created God? Where is heaven? When will my prayer take effect? " " Besides, I want my children to know that I consider religion important," says another mother. Some wives are worried about their husbands. " My husband is not a confessed Christian. He has never been to a church since we got married. I try to somehow ' witness ' my faith. He is willing to listen and talk, but when he asks questions I just don't know how to answer them. He is just too smart. It's time for me to learn."

Still another group that deserves our attention includes those who simply desire to know and who value knowledge for its own sake. The impelling motive is curiosity, as if they are committed to wanting to learn. Their intellect compels them to investigate a subject. They attend study groups mainly to learn about Christianity. These are mentally equipped, interested, curious, and sometimes spiritually alert people, and may be described, in the words of Thomas Huxley, as those who are willing to face the fact " as a little child."

Many adults who are decisively and directly oriented to the " good old days " or " the old-time religion " join study groups to confirm their piety and moralism. They are interested more in the cult of reassurance that all is well with the world than in facing the disturbing message of the gospel. Others come to learn something about religion in general but shy away from the authentic Biblical faith; still others are anxious to learn how to be Christian but they have little interest in an intellectual grappling with serious problems of life and death.

Optimistic adults are eager to learn how to solve life's problems and be happy. Sometimes this is a question of religious naïveté, and sometimes a confusion between moralism and faith. But beyond the superficial, one can detect a real struggle for meaning and a sincere quest for truth.

Among the above-mentioned groups there are a few " un-churched " people who consider themselves unbelievers, heretics, and rebels. They argue, they disagree, and they challenge the validity of the Christian faith, sometimes with well-informed and intelligent sincerity and sometimes with bitterness and sarcasm. They believe they have something important to say to church groups and are eager to have their point of view heard and appreciated. Most of these people attend classes quite regularly and once in a while ad-mit that the discussions have been helpful and stimulating. What are the motivations of these people and what are the factors that keep them coming? To argue and air their griev-ances, prejudices, and hurts? Maybe. To be in a group where they can be heard and known as intellectuals, nonconform-ists, and free from hypocrisy? Perhaps. Experience has shown that the very nature of this type of behavior is an in-dication that people are grasping for a religious outlook on life, and are seeking answers to the most important questions of life. Furthermore, their regular attendance may be an in-dication of their hope that someday, somehow, they will be able to come to an understanding of what life is and ought to be, and that maybe this is the place and the time when it can happen.

Thus, adults join study groups because they have numer-ous problems, tragedies and triumphs, joys and sorrows that cannot be dismissed as though they do not exist. There are so many things they would like to be able to understand. They look for meaning; they try to relate their questions to what they feel is within their own minds and souls. In the meantime, we are not forgetting the scientist who says: " Don't tell me what man can and cannot know. Tell me how I can have faith." The sophisticated believer knows that he could be wrong, so he is ready to listen and hear more. The legalist wants to learn of the good life by news of a code of conduct. These and many more are asking the basic ques-tions with which Christianity concerns itself.

When all the reasons have been piled up and sifted, two points must be made clear.

First, whatever the reasons for joining study groups, and however superficial, however sentimental and pious they may be, this upsurge of interest in Christian adult education must be acknowledged to be a valid groping for ultimate meaning. Regardless of the motive, the consciousness of religious poverty is a sign that laymen are aware of the fact that there are basic questions in life, and that the life more abundant is a possibility.

Secondly, whatever the nature of Christian adult education, and regardless of its ambiguous purposes and inadequate practices, the fact remains that these groups have made clear something that has never been properly acknowledged by the church, namely, that most Christians have a dim sense of the actual meaning of their Christian faith, and many of them are dissatisfied and disturbed by this spiritual immaturity. The fact that few have an idea of where they stand and whether Christianity has something to offer indicates how small is the Christian remnant of informed, practicing, and hopeful believers within the mass of mere nominal Christianity.

The above descriptions may well agree with that of Saint Hereticus of *Christianity and Crisis,* who suggests in " The Churchman's Coloring Book " how to draw and color the pictures that fit the descriptions of a layman:

I'm what they call The Average Intelligent Layman.
Everybody writes books for me.
Everybody says I'm the one the church must reach.
Everybody says the future of Protestantism lies in my
    hands.
Wow!
I blush to say that I can't understand the books.
Color me red.
I blanch when I admit that the church isn't reaching me.

Color me white.
I'm depressed about the future of Protestantism.
Color me blue.
I'm what they call the Average Intelligent Layman.
Color me red, white, and blue.[1]

In Chapters I and II we shall gain a clearer picture of who these adults are and why they believe as they do. But first we shall turn our attention to the questions they ask and the answers they seek.

◇ I ◇

QUESTIONS ADULTS ASK

Adults ask all kinds of questions. Some are asked as the quest for meaning is challenged by the message of the Christian faith; others rise from the existential experience of people; and still others are asked out of the search for truth in the sphere of human knowledge and experience. These are the people who, as Denbeaux says, show enough humility to risk communication, who express their dependency without being too proud to beg or to share, and " who dared to hope even when they could not understand." [2]

In what follows, it must be insisted that we have neither the space nor the intention to make a comprehensive survey of the questions laymen ask. Rather, the aim is to describe various ways adults raise their questions and the kind of answers they seek to their problems. Obviously we can do no more than touch upon a few vital issues. The full purpose of this chapter will be realized if the reader is at least made aware of the variety and complexity of questions, the circumstances under which they are asked, and the presuppositions that prompt them.

Two further remarks need to be added to clarify the nature of this discussion. First, we can scarcely consider the conversations that took place in these groups as question-answer schemes in the form of a catechism. To do so is to do violence to the nature of the discussion itself and to the purpose of Christian education, which is to encourage adults to seek answers to their own questions. Secondly, we do not in-

tend to appy Tillich's " method of correlation " by adjusting
the Christian message to the situation and hence fitting its
answers to the questions asked. Tillich has developed his
method in the first volume of his *Systematic Theology,* where
he points out that his method " tries to correlate the questions implied in the situation with the answers implied in the
message." [3] This means that when man asks ultimate questions — the meaning of his own existence, of what it means to
be as over against not to be — he opens his life to God's
revelation of himself. The message of the gospel comes as an
answer to man's ultimate questions. The human need and
divine revelation find their correlation in their very nature.

Christian educators are particularly concerned with questions laymen ask because the character of their work depends
upon the guidance they give in identifying and clarifying
issues. Granted Tillich's method of correlation is helpful in
this respect, it is not so simple as it looks. Those who have
found it congenial to the function of Christian education need
to have a clear understanding of it and to be fully aware of
the problems it raises.

Having said this, we now move to the purpose of this chapter, namely, what kind of questions adults ask and what
these questions reveal about the nature of their faith as
Christians and as churchgoing members.

First, we have pointed out that some questions adults ask
rise out of intellectual struggle for truth and meaning. But
who are the " intellectuals "? They are people from all
walks of life: scientists, lawyers, teachers, psychologists,
politicians, musicians, social workers, physicians, engineers,
nurses, clerks, barbers, homemakers, and the plain folks who
think and ask, " What is this all about? " Among them are
the intellectually elite who raise serious questions for our
thinking. They confront us with philosophical and scientific
problems as well as with Biblical and theological questions.
They challenge us to see the relation between intellectual life
and Christian living, between speculative inquiries of de-

tached minds and the practical reasoning of the existing person. They force us to take ontology and epistemology seriously and encourage us to employ our deepest intellectual understanding. The social scientist wants to understand the nature of the basic person. The philosopher or the philosophically minded layman asks whether the Christian faith has that uniting principle of truth by which he can understand all the various concepts and opinions that are available.

To be more specific, there are those, especially among young people, who would like to believe, provided the existence of God could somehow be proved as a proposition of science. Although the philosophical proofs of the existence of God are abstract demonstrations and are hardly convincing proof, some of these young people admit that they are helped by such arguments because they point to the mysterious character of life and the need to discover ultimate meanings. Some say these arguments help them reach an understanding of God, who becomes the objectified God of metaphysics, but they frankly admit that this God is far from the God they read about in the Bible. Furthermore, they are not willing to stop with definitions that describe God in impersonal terms, but are anxious to continue their search. " That is why I'm here," said a young man, " to find out what others say." Most of these younger folks believe there is some kind of basic order and reality in nature and human life, but only a few are anxious to ask: " How can I know this Reality, and what is he like? " or, " How is this Reality concerned with human beings — with me? " A more serious question was put as follows: " Do I have to believe in a personal God in order to call myself Christian? " In still another case, it was agreed by a few that the Roman Catholic teachings are more challenging and satisfying to the mind than the Protestant.

The shocks of biology remain unresolved for many. Some are still bothered by the conflict between the idea of Creator God and the scientific account of evolution. " It scares me to think that I must look back to a long line of apelike ancestors." We are constantly reminded that biology unites man intimately with the world of nature, but the more man is informed of this unity, the more frightened he is when he discovers that these laws apply to him. Those who are involved in this predicament wonder how it is possible to reconcile the findings of biology with the idea that man was created in God's image.

Or take another group of laymen. We know that only a small minority among adults is active in science, but a good number of them form their ideas about what is true and untrue, certain and uncertain, according to what they remember from high school days or what they read in popular literature or even what they hear from their children. And they seem dissatisfied with things as they are. They ask for causes and proofs; they want to be able to know something about everything.

The foregoing discussion brings us to the second point, namely, that those who are engaged in intellectual questioning of faith do so not necessarily by abstract thinking but through a serious examination of their daily existence and the relevance to themselves of the Christian ideas of God, sin, Christ, and salvation. Their questions are practical and personal in nature rather than speculative in form. Sometimes they are the product of the tradition in which the person was reared, and sometimes the result of a personal wrestling with problems of life's meaning in general.

In this connection it is important to recognize that there are certain questions of almost universal concern that have been asked for centuries without producing universally accepted answers. These questions deal with the ultimate meaning of life, and men of each era have continued to ask them within the context of their human knowledge and experience without arriving at final and conclusive answers. A number of laymen are familiar with the traditional content of the Christian faith, but they are also aware of the fact that no generation inherits these ideas as settled truths that require no further inquiry. Furthermore, they believe that the challenges of this century are different and so seemingly require different answers. Therefore, it is their right to bring out their questions frankly and firmly into the open and discuss them. In the following pages we shall describe these questions briefly. Some of them represent long-continued emphases and concerns. But all of them are important in offering glimpses into the question of why adults believe as they do.

QUESTIONS ABOUT GOD

From childhood most adults have heard and learned various descriptions and explanations of God. Some adults are vague and naïve; some are childish, primitive, and even bizarre. It is often obvious that by asking questions, they either repudiate these ideas or are seriously anxious to come to a better understanding of God and his relation to man.

Let us venture to say that the point is not that most adults want to know God, but rather that they want to know *about* God in order to " correct " their belief and hence pass the test of being a Christian. " How else will I know about God unless someone tells me who he is! " " The Christian God — who is he? People give so many different definitions and yet call themselves Christian. I want to know the right definition! "

To be sure, abstract definitions of God are either too broadly or too narrowly understood. The more abstract the term, the more varied is the individual's definition of its meaning. For instance, concepts of God as power, love, and righteousness are often understood anthropomorphically in terms of time and space. Sometimes the problem is more serious when human symbols about God, such as father, judge, shepherd, etc., are taken too literally. " If God is a loving Father, how can he be a judge at the same time? " " If God is all-powerful, why doesn't he make people do his will? " " Could we substitute another name for Shepherd? "

Often one gets the impression that adults speak of God as " something " to be talked or written about, and many times he is just an idea somewhere in a person's imagination.

One further note may be useful with respect to such inquiry, namely, there are always the questions: " What does it mean to have trust in God? " " How do we know what God says to us in a given situation? " " How do we know his will? " " How can I teach my children to have faith in God? "

Some laymen, instead of asking objective questions about God and his will for the world, question their own understanding of God. " I don't deny that God exists, but what troubles me is I think of him only when I am in church or when I say my prayers. The rest of the time it is as if he is not there, and I forget him," says a young woman anxiously. Could we say that this is another way of seeking for God or that such an experience opens up man's restless quest for God? This is not to say that God is found by searching. Christian faith is man's response to God's revelation of himself in Jesus Christ. What is happening here is that this young woman begins to question her own understanding of God. The question may bring her to an encounter with God in faith.

The following conversation describes how adults run away from God without knowing that they do:

" Why is it that sometimes I don't want to know about God? "

" Well, it is like your conscience. When it warns you against something or when it pesters you, you are scared. You become apprehensive, so you run away from it."

" But I don't run away from God. On the contrary. I want to know him! "

" Maybe you feel this way when you have to make a decision? "

" When you run away from what you are supposed to do, you are running away from God."

" Next time, I'm really going to force myself to find out

why I feel the way I do, because it's a very uncomfortable feeling."

Some adults ask for a few answers or explanations about God and are not willing to accept the fact that there always will be much more they do not experience or understand. They find it disturbing to face the different conceptions of God in the Bible, especially in the Old Testament. " I get more confused with all these ideas. Isn't there a simple answer? " asks a frightened adult. But there are also those who, realizing the value of various explanations, nevertheless raise the question of how one decides what is acceptable and what is not acceptable. " I know nobody can decide for me, but I still would like to know on what basis I should make my decision." Those who are never satisfied with what they already know or experience search for more concepts to explain the mystery of life, for they say, " The more I know about life, the clearer my understanding of God becomes."

Questions about prayer are common and varied. Some are naïve and childish, and others show considerable maturity. The great majority admit to a more or less regular use of prayer; for some it is a habit: "After all, all Christians pray " (they don't say, " Good people pray "!), and for others it is an obligation: " All Christians are supposed to pray. Jesus said so."

According to what some adults report, prayer rises out of their anxiety. " When I get frantic, I pray." Or, " I just need some help from someone when I get desperate, so I pray. Is this wrong? " There are those who are a little worried because they have an idea that their prayer life is not what it is supposed to be. " I don't consciously pray — I don't use words or I don't talk with God. It is just a feeling I have. It is just a mood. Would you say this is not Christian? "

Often utilitarian ideas are confused with spiritual life. For instance, some ask how to pray to get relief and comfort in times of stress and crisis, or, better still, how to pray " to get something out of it." More sophisticated people are anxious to know whether it is right to pray for happiness, success, and safety. " Is it ethical to pray to win the cold war? " someone asks.

" There was no doubt that John Glenn would return from his orbital flight because so many people were praying for him," says a church school teacher, " and I told my Sunday school girls that." " The reason why God doesn't answer prayers is that we don't say the right things. But how do we know whether we have said the right words or not? " These questions and many others similar to them reveal the fact that many people cannot avoid regarding the relative efficacy of prayer as some kind of " wonder drug." " After all, the more you pray, the better off you are," comments one man. " But I never know whether my prayer is effective or not," adds another.

Enough examples have been given to show that the motives for prayer are various and complex, and it is not too far from the mark to say that these are the symptoms of a prayer life that is basically diffuse. However, we do not lose hope; those who are really struggling with faith and unfaith are eager to be able to pray. They ask how they can make their petitions and intercessions in accordance with God's will.

That these remarks say nothing different from what we already know may be so obvious that our reporting seems unnecessary. Yet the fact that they were spoken under circumstances that allowed them to be expressed openly may caution us against assuming hastily that they are as commonplace as they seem. The legacy of " ask, and it will be given you " has been so much with us that a clear grasp of how adults interpret its implications is not only necessary but imperative.

Closely connected with this attitude toward prayer is that of adults who claim that they find answers to their questions through intuition. Here is an adult who sincerely believes that important knowledge (especially moral) comes to man in some form of immediate awareness.

" When I want to find out which denomination is more right than the others I go to different ministers, and each tries to prove that his is the best. I know the guidepost is Jesus Christ, but I also know that there are different interpretations of him, so how can I tell? I depend on my own intuition. There is a special apprehension that comes to me through meditation and prayer. Is this wrong? "

We are calling the attention of the reader to this particular case because this woman was denied membership in one of the major denominations on the basis that such knowledge (intuition) is the product of ordinary secular intelligence rather than spiritual insight.

The most challenging questions rise out of the experience of frustration, meaninglessness, and the ultimate limitations of existence. Here is a man whose experience of life seems only to pose more questions instead of answering those he has already asked. He has come to the end of his moral and spiritual resources and asks whether God has anything at all to do with his life. " Is life really worth living? What is the meaning of life? When I honestly and deeply face my life, then I know I have nothing to hope for, and this frightens me! " He doubts God's faithfulness, " Sometimes it's as if you don't want to face the fact that God really exists. At times everything seems hopeless, and I want to give up! "

Those who ask the question in personal terms such as, " What is the purpose of my life in these difficult days? " find it easier to comprehend what the Christian faith says than those who ask the question in an impersonal way, " What is the purpose of life? "

The pragmatist and the idealist have their own way of looking at life. Some do not care whether there is purpose in life or not. " What difference does it make? " they ask. Others are not even interested enough to ask, and when the answer is given, they do not comprehend what is being said. The idea that the universe is the result of God's purposeful activity sounds vague. " If that is the case, then, how do we find its purpose? " some ask. " If there is purpose in the world, then why so much poverty, injustice, and war? "

QUESTIONS ABOUT EVIL

The problem of evil and suffering haunts almost every thinking adult. They want to understand the nature of good in life and find some kind of solution to the problem of evil. This problem of reconciling the existence of evil with the goodness of God is an old one and has been familiar at least since the time of Job. Yet with the advance of knowledge and the complications of modern life it seems to become more difficult. In regard to this matter a few observations should be made.

First, people want answers (sometimes intellectual answers) to questions of suffering, pain, and evil. For instance, questions about God's omnipotence and his relation to the world are quite common. The perennial questions are: " If God is good and can do anything he wants to, why does he not prevent suffering, war, and tragedy? " " Why did God allow the destruction of six million Jews? " " Why does he allow the evil to prosper? " " Why do innocent people suffer? " It is incomprehensible, they say, that the good God should allow his creatures to suffer and die in agony. What about the deformed and the idiot child? What about those who go through their whole existence sick through no fault of their own?

It must be observed that those who ask for rational analysis of these problems remain unsatisfied with intellectual answers, and rightly so. " What is said makes sense, but I'm still puzzled," they say.

Secondly, problems dealing with practical concern in respect to everyday life become more intense when adults themselves are existentially faced with tragedy, suffering, and death. " How can you have faith when you know your son is going to die of leukemia? " " How is faith possible when you have experienced the sudden and unexpected loss of a loved one? " " Is there really a future life, or is it a projection of a person's wishful thinking? "

Some questions recognize the factor of mystery. For instance, granted that some adults understand the accidental and mysterious part of natural evil such as famine, earthquake, disease, and various accidents, they still ask, " Why did it have to happen to the only child? " Or, " Why did the plane crash take the life of my husband, who was on a goodwill mission? "

Thirdly, the extreme forms of human evil — murder, physical and mental torture, exploitation, especially where clearly motivated by hate, lust for power, and sadistic desire — raise the question, " Why does not God stop inhumanity? "

The following piece of conversation will clarify our point:

" The fact that we have all these cruelties (the slaughter of Jews) is the best proof that the world hasn't gotten any better."

" This was just one man's doing — an insane man like Hitler — but it doesn't mean that the world is full of people like him."

" We always see the dark side of life. Look at all the improvement in the world — in education, economics."

" There are good things, but the good and evil are increasing every day no matter how hard we try. We spend money and effort to bring justice to nations, but our wars are getting bigger and more dangerous."

" It seems there will always be evil in the world no matter how hard we try."

" Does this mean that man is basically bad and that there is no hope for him? "

" Was man created this way? "

" If man is basically evil, then there is no hope for the world? "

" I don't know why we should look at Hitler or Khrushchev. Why don't we look at ourselves? Most of our social, economic, and political decisions are selfish and are in the interest of our own nation. All these accumulate, and someday they will plunge us into another world war."

This brings us to our fourth observation, namely, that it is important to listen to answers adults give as reasons for evil and suffering in the world because such answers raise further questions.

Some consider suffering as punishment for sin or for not having " obeyed God's will." Others look at it as simply a test of one's faith in God. They say, " It helps us grow." The former express pious religious sentiment and ask how to know and do "what God wants of us "; the latter evade the issue and fail to understand clearly how suffering can have a healing quality about it and how resources have been made available to us by the " good news."

Somehow or other both groups make God responsible for evil and suffering. Some realize man's abuse of freedom and admit, " It is not God's fault if we choose wrongly "; others show lack of discrimination between types of suffering and pain, and moral law; and still others justify evil by completely evading it.

In conclusion, adults report that it is not easy to have faith. Some admit that it comes in time of genuine and profound disturbances in the self. What they mean is that faith and crisis go hand in hand. Time and again they admit that only when they faced death, guilt, struggle, or suffering did they become aware of the narrowness and superficiality of their accustomed way of looking at the world and were prompted to ask questions. Only in experiencing the limitations of their existence did they recognize the transitoriness of the cause in which they had put their trust and so discover their dependence upon an objective power beyond themselves. What shall we think about those who say that in their desperate struggle *against* God they experienced what God really is? The questions that these men and women ask are the questions that the Christian faith is attempting to answer.

QUESTIONS ABOUT JESUS CHRIST

The question, Who is Jesus Christ? is the most serious question adults ask. Questions about the nature of Christ and of the process by which one arrives at a decision about him are difficult, numerous, and complex. To be sure, these problems are not new; they are the questions of the early church and they will continue to be asked whenever Christians confront themselves by confronting Him. The following excerpt from a discussion will give the reader a glimpse of what adults believe and know about the nature of Jesus Christ and the kinds of questions they ask.

" My understanding is that Jesus was the best man who ever lived. Call him the greatest teacher or the greatest prophet if you wish. If everybody follows him and does what he teaches, believe me, this world will be a better place in which to live."

" What do you mean when you say he was the best man, or he was perfect? There must have been some reason for being great or best or perfect; besides, how do you decide what best or perfect is? "

" He was different from the rest of us in the degree of his goodness and perfection."

" You mean someday someone will reach his perfection? "

" It is hard to tell. Why rule out such a possibility? "

" Then what about his divinity? Isn't this the most important thing about Jesus? "

" If by divinity you mean he was God, this I don't accept."

" It means he was God and man at the same time. And if

Christians don't believe in this, then what is left? Why not follow someone else? "

" By divinity I mean God was working through him to show himself to man. Of course this happens to us too, but more so in Jesus."

" When I say Jesus was divine, I mean he had no sin."

" What do you mean by sin? "

" He always obeyed God. He was God's beloved Son. He loved everyone, even his enemies. He knew everything and could do everything."

" Does that make him God? "

" His miracles prove his divinity."

" Is it necessary to believe Jesus was divine? "

" If you don't believe in the divinity of Jesus, does that mean you are not a Christian? "

" If one doesn't believe that Jesus shows us who God is and what we must be, then, I believe, he is missing the greatest teaching of the Christian faith."

" He also shows us who we are."

" The point is not whether you accept this or not; it is whether this really happens to you when you read or think about Jesus."

All that we have said brings us to the following observations. Many of our laymen are anxious to establish the full humanity of Jesus in their minds by considering him the best teacher, the greatest prophet, and the ideal man whom they should and could imitate. There are those who protest quite vigorously against the concept of Jesus Christ being truly human and truly divine. This is because, they say, the idea of incarnation does not fit in with modern knowledge. Some even consider it narrow, ridiculous, and insulting to their intelligence. There are those who cannot make up their minds. Those who do realize the mystery of it are in search of more enlightenment. And only a small minority can talk about it experientially. Nevertheless, questions like: " How can I decide whether God was in Christ? " " How do I know God has revealed himself to man fully in Christ? " " Just how was God in Jesus? " " Why did God reveal himself in Jesus and not in someone else? " " What does it mean to have faith in Christ? " are serious questions, and, granting that they are very difficult to understand, the challenge is how to interpret them and make them meaningful to adults.

It is fair to say that these problems are shared by ministers, and laymen know it and are disturbed by it. A layman put the matter rather bluntly: " Our minister accepts Jesus as a perfect man and is quite willing to refer to him as Master, but when I ask him why he rejects Jesus' divinity, he says he doesn't reject it but that the claims cancel each other. Is this true? "

QUESTIONS ABOUT CROSS AND RESURRECTION

We have noted briefly how puzzling and difficult adults find the question, " Who is Jesus? " but let us hasten to add that the meaning of the cross and resurrection are just as difficult, if not more so. Although the two doctrines cannot be separated theologically, for the sake of clarity we shall discuss them separately. First, then, let us find out what laymen know about the meaning of the cross.

There are subtle ways of acknowledging the cross without really coming face to face with its dynamic power. For instance, many people refer to some suffering that cannot be escaped, such as the sudden death of loved ones, sudden loss of health, or even loss of property and wealth, as " bearing my cross." Often such a statement reveals the capacity for self-pity, and many times it is a sign of passive acceptance of life's tragedies. There is a strange devaluation of the real meaning of the cross when adults ask, " How shall I gain strength to bear suffering? " " Does it mean that because Jesus bore his suffering, I should too? " " Doesn't it mean that I should accept life's tragedies without any complaints? " They do not realize that " bearing the cross " means giving one's self to the requirements and for the sake of God's Kingdom.

In the second place, adults refuse the real meaning of the cross while all the time they seem to espouse it. For instance, there is no difficulty in accepting the fact that Jesus died for the highest ideals or that the cross was the price he paid for his courage. The idea that the cross shows Jesus' perfect love to men and his faithfulness to God's demands is also given verbal acceptance without realizing the relation of the cross to its consequences in human life and character. Here is an ethical human being who is worthy of being acknowledged — and even of being worshiped, if you will.

Modern Christians are not reluctant to accept the cross as an example. " When I look at the cross, I remember that I should love my fellowmen and even my enemies." " But why doesn't this happen to everybody? " asks a thoughtful person.

Having said this about where adults stand in their understanding of the meaning of the cross, we shall turn our attention to the question, " Why was Jesus put to death? " This is another way of asking, " What is the meaning of Jesus' death? " As we shall see in the next chapters, even though few people are willing to comprehend the tragic conclusion of *why*, the question is asked consistently and stubbornly. Some satisfy their curiosity by accepting reasons such as: " He died because his death was foretold in the Old Testament." " Good people are never appreciated. They are usually rejected, but later they realize their mistakes, and sometimes it is too late." " Almost every life has its tragic moments."

A great number of adults readily and proudly answer the question by saying, " He died for our sins." But the truth of the matter is that when this statement is probed for meaning, the result is mysterious mumbo-jumbo phrases. One of the reasons why many adults have no use for the doctrine of atonement is probably the use of ancient theological language that has lost its symbolic meaning. Phrases such as " the lamb of God " and " the precious blood " that have become the stock-in-trade of Christian preaching are considered crude and old-fashioned. Some who are vaguely familiar with various interpretations of the doctrine of atonement reject it on the ground that it is archaic, cruel, and meaningless for our age.

The question, " Who killed Jesus? " is asked cautiously and in a subtle manner lest it offend Jewish friends or be labeled anti-Semitic. While some wrestle with historic facts, others accuse the " bad " Romans and the " bad " Jews who killed Jesus.

But if Jesus died for our sins, " What is sin? " We shall deal with this question in the following pages; here, suffice it to say that adults usually think of sin in terms of sins and wrongdoings and ask if some sins are more serious than others. Sometimes questions about sin emerge when the person becomes aware of the conflict that lies between the resistance that is deep within him and his will to self-realization. Many laymen are dissatisfied with life in general. They are anxious to know what prevents life from being good, true, and beautiful. Most of these questions are specific and concrete rather than general and vague. " I try very hard, but it is as if someone, something, always pulls me in the wrong direction. I know there is something wrong inside me. Is this what you call sin? There is always some kind of resistance that prevents me from being what I want to be. I don't know what it is," explains a worried adult.

Those who are overcome by the depth of their guilt, haunted by self-pity, despairing because life has lost meaning for them, ask the most searching questions about sin and salvation. Some few ask about the causes of misery, anxiety, tyrannical conscience, crime, race prejudice, economic injustice, and war.

Is there any connection between sin and death in the minds of adults? The answer is, " Not at all." Without presuming to give a detailed analysis, we may briefly state what adults think of death and what kind of questions they ask.

Let us remind ourselves that there are those who avoid the crucial question of death or ask the question without being certain that they really want an answer. This is not because people accept death as trivial or incidental, but because they are awed by its reality and feel an inner poverty before it. Modern man lives in a culture that evades and conceals the pain of death. " I don't ask about death because I don't know what to ask." " The time when I really became aware of the horror of death was when I lost my son." " The first time I started to think about death was when my little daughter asked why people die." " All I can say about death is that it destroys life's meaning for me, so what is there to say? "

Here we do not intend to forget those who accept death as the will of God. For some, this is a sincere and courageous belief, for others a sentimental and pious statement. Many believe that there should be a life for those who have suffered grievous wrongs or for whom the enjoyment of life is denied here; therefore, death is a blessing.

People who openly admit that they are afraid of death are those who are threatened by separation from flesh and their loved ones. This kind of fear is perhaps aggravated by our rituals and ceremonies that are characterized by a desperate effort to evade the presence of death. " I don't know how to express my feelings about death — with tears or with smiles. Do we confront ourselves with the idea that everybody is going to die, or with the thought that there is a better life waiting for us beyond death? " asks a layman who has gone through tragic experiences of suffering and death.

But death also threatens man with separation from God. This is the horror of death that men do not fully face, and the question of how " he descended into hell " remains partly rhetorical because they do not fully know what they ask and because they have never fully experienced the present possibility of new life that God offers in Christ and for which they may decide. Instead, they have theoretical and speculative interests in the incarnation, the cross, the resurrection, and the second coming and judgment. They attempt to reach an objective understanding of what happened on Easter Day. They look for historical and scientific evidences of the resurrection appearances. They ask why there should be any difference between the experiences of the disciples and those of later Christians, including ourselves. Confusion is caused by attempting to reduce the problem to modern man's ideas of time and space.

Some ask how to decide what they should believe about the resurrection. Here we may assume that they either ignore their own experience of God, no matter how dim, or think in terms of a certain set of ideas to be believed intellectually. Having said this, let us also add that there are still those who sincerely ask: " What does it mean to have the experience of the living Christ? " " What is meant by ' in Christ '? " " What does it mean that God reconciles us? " " Will goodness win at the end? " " Why is it important for a Christian to believe in the resurrection? "

We will do well to remember also the age-old questions: " Is there life after death? " " What is going to happen after death? " " Is there really life after death — what kind? " " How do we know? " " The reason why so many people go to church on Easter is that they want to know what will happen to them after death," says a layman. " First they think about themselves, then they are curious to know what happened to Jesus," adds another.

In spite of faithful attendance at Easter Day services and hearing sermons year after year, the majority of laymen have the vague notion that the " spirit continues to live after death." " I have a feeling that it would," says one with assurance. Many have non-Christian views of immortality such as the absorption theory or reincarnation. They are shocked and hurt when their ideas of immortality in the

Platonic sense of the word are challenged or corrected. Thus, the question, " What is the future life? " remains a perennial one.

Belief in immortality is often held for self-centered reasons: " We must be good in this life in order to be happy in the future life." " This life is a preparation for future life in which there will be happiness and even perfection." " I believe in the future life because I want to see my family and be with them."

In the foregoing paragraphs, we have attempted to show the most widely shared questions and interpretations about Jesus Christ among modern laymen. Some of them may sound superficial, others are naïve and refined varieties of literalism, and still others are misconceptions and incomprehensible thoughts. But when all this has been said, let us also acknowledge the fact that these and a host of similar questions often are the result of honest minds trying to understand the full implications of the meaning of Jesus Christ. An alert, rigorous, and searching faith is eager to wrestle with these problems because intellect and experience demand it, and it is only the lazy and self-complacent mind that ignores such questions and considers them a waste of time.

QUESTIONS ABOUT THE CHURCH

Many adults find that the old traditions which long gave security to life have lost their meaning. They bluntly admit that Christian words and symbols no longer convey the meanings they were intended to, so they ask for explanations and clarifications of terms like " the body of Christ."

People have vague ideas about the sacraments of the church. A layman put the matter succinctly: " To be quite frank, the Holy Communion has lost its meaning for me. I have taken it for granted for such a long time. Now I want to find out what it means, why it is so important, and what values it has for me personally." This problem is shared by many laymen. Here is a very intelligent person who tries hard to emancipate himself from something he thinks is dead, mechanical, and impersonal. He is one of the many who raise questions about the meaning of worship and its essential elements. " I don't know what it means to worship. The sermons are above my head; I don't understand them. Why go to church anyway? " This is the confession of someone who seldom goes to church but attends study groups quite regularly. " I like this," he says, " because I learn something."

" Individual religion " is often intensified by the rugged individualism of many American laymen. Those who prefer " individual Christianity " want to stay home, hear a sermon on the radio, and, if need be, shovel the neighbor's sidewalk!

Common in these days are the " angry young men," a small but significant number who frankly and boldly question the value of the institutionalized church. Sometimes their questions represent disillusionment engendered by visible hypocrisy and failure in the organized church. They want to know what the gospel has to say about moral issues and how they can be implemented in effective justice. They claim that the church does not relate its message to the wear and tear of everyday life. They question the heavy silence of the church about racial and social injustices and exploitation in the world about them. They are puzzled about the indifference and placidity of Christians who talk but don't act. Aware of superficial social niceties in church life coupled with a lack of social concern for human life, they are quite cynical about " Christian charity " which encourages a generous contribution to the church budget that includes a Hungarian or a Cuban refugee family. They are bothered by the occupation of the church with the trivial: fairs, dinners, bazaars, when the world is hanging on the rim of disaster. Thus the serious question, "How can we make up our minds where we stand on a church? " is asked by sensitive adults.

Realizing all this, we can make the following comments:

First, it is obvious that some people in the church are aware of the church's preoccupation with false piety and ask whether it stands for or against God.

Secondly, some criticize the church because they have no idea what Christianity is all about. Their challenge is an indication of a quest for meaning in regard to the nature and the mission of the church.

Granting, then, that this is the case, the question that faces us is, What can be said to these laymen to clarify the meaning of the church? Or, better still, are we willing to say to these laymen that their indictment of the church is not severe enough, provided they also see its potential greatness?

QUESTIONS ABOUT THE FUTURE

Today more than ever American Protestants are conscious of the world at large and are asking: " What is going to happen? " " Where are we heading? " The anxiety of the nuclear dilemma and the threat of possible annihilation in the event of another world war has intensified the questions and made people keenly aware of the problem of history. They want to know what is beyond the end mostly in terms of time and space rather than in terms of the fulfillment of God's sovereignty.

In spite of the space age, some are still concerned about the geography of heaven and hell and the Kingdom's boundaries. " When will the Last Judgment come and what is it like? " " Will there be some kind of accounting for our deeds? " " Will Hitler and Schweitzer be judged in the same way? " " What about those who have never heard of God? Will they be judged too? " " What about non-Christians? What will happen to them? " " What are the signs of the second coming of Christ? "

Few realize that they need to do more than look to the unknown future and ask how they can be freed for responsible and courageous living. " We must do our best here and now and leave the rest in God's hands," some say. Those who are aware of the Age of Suspicion would like to know how they can tell what things are really important and need doing. They are anxious to develop a sense of discrimination in making decisions and fighting for worthy causes. The life of Christians behind the Iron Curtain and the heroic accounts of Christian resistance under various kinds of persecution prompt the question, " How can I tell whether my faith is able to bear me up under persecution if and when it comes? "

In summary, what these statements mean is that these laymen are asking one of the most important questions, namely, the meaning of eschatological faith. We do not assert, of course, that everybody is equally disturbed by the crisis in which the world is immersed. The American habit is to be optimistic even in the face of cataclysm. The end of time and what it is like is not important. Some Christians are less disturbed than others, and they would rather leave the question of when the end will come and what it is like to Jehovah's Witnesses to answer.

QUESTIONS ABOUT ETHICS

As we listen to ethical questions laymen ask, we are immediately struck by the great variety of positions that people hold and the complexity of the question of right and wrong. In this section we will not attempt to review the whole problem of the relation of the Christian faith to ethics, for such an attempt would double the length of the book. One task is to present the ways in which the ethical problems are formulated by adults. To this end, we shall try to understand the presuppositions that initiate the questions, and more particularly, we shall listen to their conversations and questions.

Two preliminary observations may help us to have a general idea before we discuss the matter in detail. In the first place, adults appear to be caught in a world where morality is inescapable. They realize that one cannot live without getting involved in making the choice between right and wrong, good and evil. Christians with serious moral concern are in deep search of some kind of basis for morality that they can really believe and live with all their heart, soul, and mind. They find themselves thinking that in spite of cultural, practical, and logical difficulties there should be some universally acceptable or, better still, Christian answers. What some hope for are Christian rules by which to settle the issues with ease and in some way for everyone alike; others ask for moral guidance in relation to concrete, personal, or social choices. In the second place, we may observe that adults are well aware of the experience of moral failure. They recognize ethical ambiguity and are aware of its deep poignancy. The fact that the problem is one of the will and not of the intellect is clear to some. The question they ask is how to engender the required motivation or how to overcome the failure of motivation.

Since ethical decisions involve what one ought to do in a certain situation, the problem of the source of the feeling of " ought " becomes serious. Further, since the adult is involved in a concrete situation, the question of the resources of ethical guidance for his moral action becomes evident. For instance, when he asks, " How do I discover what I must do? " he does not intend to invent an answer but to discover the right answer. He is hesitant about freely choosing from among existing possibilities; therefore, he is anxious to go to the source — the Bible — to discover resources for ethical guidance. In other words, he wants to " think Biblically " about life. Here are some samples:

> " It is true that the Ten Commandments and the ethical teachings of Jesus do not produce love of God and love of neighbor in us, but at least we know we are given guidance, and we can control our irresponsibilities."
>
> " As far as I'm concerned, the Sermon on the Mount is really what morals are all about, and we must be able to live by it."
>
> " That is impossible. But the Sermon does remind us how

we have failed in our responsibilities, and this in itself is a good beginning."

" Yes, at least we are able to see the difference between good and bad, right and wrong, Christian and unchristian."

" To be truthful, the teachings of Jesus upset me instead of comforting me. They're too ideal! "

" I would rather see the Ten Commandments on the wall of the United Nations Security Hall than a painting that nobody, not even the artist himself, knows what it is about. At least the Ten Commandments will remind the nations of their responsibilities."

" The best they can do is to sensitize their consciences."

" I don't care what you say, I still think the Ten Commandments and even the teachings of Jesus should not and cannot be taken literally. The demands are impossibly high. My question is, How can we apply them to everyday life? "

Thus, many laymen, including some sideline Christians, would like to know the implications of Jesus' ethic for the issues of marriage, divorce, war, nonviolence, etc. Many of them are just beginning to realize the importance of their involvement in life, especially in politics. " Why should a Christian enter the field of politics? " they ask. " Does he take a different line because he is a Christian? "

A small number of people are eager to be discriminating in their choices as they make political, economic, educational, and domestic commitments. They know that they live in a non-Christian world that does not accept the Christian ethic, and yet they must live as Christians. They are well aware of the difficulty of ethical decisions in a technological, urbanized culture that tends to dehumanize man. They know that the morality of personal value is either discouraged or even nonexistent. Nevertheless, people continue asking ethical questions that demand ethical answers. A morally sensitive scientist who disapproves of the results and consequences of his labors looks for a way to solve the tension between professional and personal ethics. Someone who works at a missile project wants to find justification for his activity; a young man is anxious to know how he can continue with his "dishonesty," which is strictly for the benefit of his company; a new college graduate is shocked by the superficiality and dishonesty of the new world he finds himself in. A typist in an insurance company is bored with her job and questions the value of her work, especially when it is done with an attitude of indifference and even defiance. A clerk in a store wonders how long she can take the dishonesty in " marking down " the prices for sale. Other questions such as: " Why should good men go to war for causes not worth fighting for? " " Is our nation truly altruistic in its aid-trade program? " " Are we as right as we believe ourselves to be? " haunt the consciences of sensitive people. In other words, they ask how it is possible to carry Christian ethic and concern into their vocation.

One of the most difficult questions that confronts people is what it means to do God's will. They want to know in advance what God wills in detail, and they ask for clear and often specific guidance that what they confidently assert is God's will is really the appropriate rule for action. " Then I won't feel at a loss as to what I should do or how I should act. Besides, I won't feel guilty about it later! "

The question, " How do I know whether I have made the right decision or not? " is asked many times and by many people. Some people like to live under a legalism that can cover the never-ending proliferation of duties and safeguard them from errors of discrimination. But those who are already caught in this plight are the Pharisees who " go about establishing their own righteousness." They ask for answers that will define the Christian life in terms of petty sins such as gambling, drinking, etc., to be avoided and petty virtues to be sought after. What they have in common is a superficial and legalistic conception of sin as man's willful failure to live up to moral laws, thus denying sin as a universal soul-destroying power that prevents men from entering into fellowship with God and man. The Biblical legalist turns the words of Jesus into a legalistic concept. He is eager to learn the rules of conduct that he thinks are outlined in the Bible, and he is in a study group to learn them. These adults would rather struggle to obey a set of externalized commands in a rote fashion than get involved in a spiritual struggle and hence be open to the creative power of the Holy Spirit.

But sometimes ethical questions are raised with the firm conviction that morality is independent of religious faith. Although occasionally God is tacked on as a label, most of the time the concept of God is waved aside as irrelevant. These people would rather be responsible to the commitments of conscience as a guide and as a prompter to good action than to God, who, after all, has more important things to do than to care whether one takes a stand for or against established institutions that support gambling and liquor. Others see education as the source for changing selfish motivations and ask how to enlighten and thus reform the greedy businessman, the selfish landlord, and the rotten politician. " If they could only understand the damage they do to the community," says a well-meaning person.

Although these people are enthusiastic about moral progress, they are naïve in their awareness of the depth of man's sin. They consider the roots of evil in human society rather simple and few. Only a few of them are aware of the fact that shallow moral reasoning, earnest emotions, and pious desires can neither educate the unconverted mind and will of the individual nor make this life the Kingdom of God on earth.

Another group of reformers is composed of those persons who are impatient with ideas and find theories rather confusing and misleading. " We are the kind of persons who need a *must* to stir us to action." They are eager to be the reformers of the world's ills, but the point is that some of them never get anything done. When it comes to action, their answer is, " Let someone else do it."

An enthusiastic P.T.A. leader calls the parents' attention to the fact that *homonoia,* the dream of Alexander the Great, has become a necessity (so she was told by an educator) and asks how the church can help. Anxious parents want to know what the church's responsibilities are in respect to school problems such as cheating, drinking, early pregnancy, etc.

A further difficulty arises from the perplexity that surrounds the problem of motivation. " If I know what is good and right, I'll have the desire for it." " I know what is good and what is right, yet I fail to want to do the good." The former wants to be enlightened by instruction; the latter wishes to know whether it is possible for the good deed and the right motivation to coincide.

To illustrate the point, we include those who put the emphasis on the act alone and evade the problem of motivation. " What must I do? " is a question that deals with conduct, not with the person who acts; in other words, it is not concerned about the motivation out of which a person acts.

" So long as I know what to do to keep a patient comfortable," says a nurse, " I'm doing my duty. My problem is what I must do rather than how I feel about it."

" How can you separate your feelings from your acts? "

" By doing good we become good; a good deed develops the habit of doing good."

" Even though this is true to a certain extent, you still must have some kind of belief that prompts the good deed."

" When I was on a jury, we all considered the motivations of the suspect. This is the most important thing."

" But our motivations are so mixed, so complex; it is not easy to know what motivates our actions."

" That's why we feel guilty all the time."

" What should we do then? "

Thus, many adults realize the fact that the inner attitude prompts the outer act, but they do not know what to do about it. They ask questions when they become aware of their accumulated guilt and frustrations as the result of repeated moral failure. " Will God forgive me? " " How should I act after I have been forgiven? " " What should I do in order to be forgiven? "

The point we have sought to develop in this chapter is the fact that all men seek some meaning of life and that this quest is revealed in the questions they ask. Further, the questions adults ask require different types of understanding. Some are in search of " knowledge about," and others in " knowledge of." In Chapter III we shall observe the important distinction of the two terms and their place in Christian education.

Why Adults Do Not Ask Questions

Christian educators show concern over the fact that some people do not and cannot ask questions. This alarm is due to the fact that learning is considered to be a completely internal process, and it is believed that it does not take place unless an individual becomes personally involved in the learning process. In other words, when a person asks questions he is involved, he is thinking, he is engaged in identifying what he wants to learn.

First, some adults do not ask or think because they hear and receive too much. This takes opposite forms in different people. On the one hand, there are those who refrain from asking serious questions when the Christian faith is presented to them in a dogmatic and authoritarian manner. Defensive appeals to faith are bound to stifle thinking and to silence questioning. An atmosphere that lacks freedom and acceptance engenders the fear of judgment and encourages uncritical silence.

On the other hand, there are those who accept certain truths " on authority." This is not to say that acceptance of certain theological truths is not valuable. As a matter of fact, it is educationally valuable to accept certain truths on authority. But the reason why so many adults respond to this kind of teaching is that it satisfies their personal need for an authoritative foundation for life upon which they can depend and feel secure. And further, they are too timid about taking intellectual risks and too fearful of getting involved in unresolved commitment, which is the mask of faith.

Secondly, " too much telling " encourages passive and dependent laymen. Many adults are too indifferent to make much of an effort to assume the responsibility of thinking for themselves. This is particularly true when they assume the passive role of a learner who does not know much and therefore is supposed to listen and learn.

Thirdly, many adults prefer the comfort of undisturbed biases rather than allowing themselves to be forced to reflect, to examine, and to reconsider their presuppositions, which is often an intolerable adventure. " I accept what I like and close my ears to what I don't like or don't agree with. So why bother to argue? "

Fourthly, some have no convictions of their own and agree with anybody who happens to be talking. They choose to enjoy the comfort of accepting opinions readily and they avoid the painful process of figuring things out for themselves. Sometimes this is a kind of infantilism partly due to the mass commercialization that informs, entertains, and comforts the public, occupying their minds much of the time with the trivial, the irrelevant, and the irrational. The adult knows he does not have to bother and so he prefers minimum intellectual effort to hard work.

After having said all this, we find it worthwhile to remember Tillich's method of correlation, which reminds the educators that " man cannot receive an answer to a question he has not asked." In other words, people hear about the answers before they feel the problem in any real sense, or, to put it even more simply, we give the answers too soon.

Finally, many intelligent people withdraw from asking serious questions when the Christian faith is presented to them in such shallowness and complacency that it seems to drain life of its mystery. These adults have a healthy distrust of simple answers and easygoing optimism because they are well aware of the complexity of life, and are conscious of the reality of its tragic element of anxiety and meaninglessness.

To close this chapter, let us make two forthright statements:

In the first place, we cannot always be satisfied with the questions laymen ask; the fact that they ignore or do not ask the basic questions of life does not mean that they do not need answers. It is therefore the function of Christian education to present and interpret the story of the Christian faith in such a way and with such conviction as to challenge those who enjoy contentment, or are untouched by ultimate questions, to ponder their own experiences and the age-old questions that lie behind the whole history of human thought and longing. The gospel message gives answers as well as asks questions. After all, it is Christ who says, " Truly, truly, I say to you, he who hears my word and believes him who sent me, has eternal life; he does not come into judgment, but has passed from death to life " (John 5:24).

In the second place, any rethinking that takes into account the importance of questions that laymen ask must be matched by its willingness to listen to answers that adults give which suggest new questions in an entirely new set of circumstances. And further, it is the function of Christian education to look more concretely at the problems that give rise to the questions rather than to transform them into questions to be answered.

◇ II ◇

BARRIERS TO FAITH

Every thinking person is likely to come across barriers as he tries to understand the meaning of the Christian faith. Even deeply committed Christians are often troubled by their inability to comprehend some of the disturbing perplexities of their faith. Adults have numerous daily problems — personal, social, political, psychological, cultural, and spiritual — which cannot be dismissed as though they were of no consequence. However, it is not the purpose of this chapter to give a detailed account of these problems and offer solutions. Both the nature of the difficulties that we intend to examine and the point of view from which we examine them are generally defined and strictly limited. Hence, no attempt has been made to discuss any single problem exhaustively, and many crucial issues have been either mentioned briefly or omitted — some purposely, others inadvertently.

The purpose of this chapter is, first, to discuss the nature of certain problems that present themselves as barriers to faith and to show how adults cope with them. Secondly, it is to encourage those who work with adults to draw the more complex theological and educational implications and to be prepared to deal with them intelligently.

Those who work with adults are well aware of the fact that the problem of faith is one of the greatest importance in Christian education. Our laymen reveal both their longing and their difficulty in believing. " Is faith possible and

how can I believe? " This is a question that is asked over
and over again either explicitly or implicitly.

But why do adults ask about the possibility of faith and
why is it difficult to understand its meaning? Or why are
they doubtful whether it really matters what they believe?
In the following pages we shall attempt to take a look at
this conflict, but first we shall begin with the problem of
faith and belief.

THE PROBLEM OF FAITH AND BELIEF

Adults find it difficult to understand the difference between
faith and belief. They believe that one has faith if he gives
his intellectual assent to certain facts and ideas or doctrines.
They identify faith with reports about faith; they substitute
intellectual propositions for faith as " the assurance of things
hoped for, the conviction of things not seen " (Heb. 11:1).
In other words, a cold, intellectual system of facts, ideas,
and doctrines becomes a guarantee of faith in the person of
Christ.

Many laymen consider themselves Christians because they
believe in certain teachings of the Bible. " I accept the Ten
Commandments; I believe in the teachings of Jesus; they
are the best we have had in the history of mankind. I don't
understand why people find it difficult to accept Christianity." Here we have someone who trusts in statements
about God and Jesus instead of having faith in the living
God of Jesus Christ who claims obedience. When " right
belief " is a substitute for faith in the God of Jesus Christ
and becomes a condition of acceptance into the church, we
hear statements like this: " I was refused membership in
the church because I could not accept their statement about
the Holy Communion."

Here we want to emphasize that faith essentially expresses
itself in articles of faith; but as William Temple says:
" Faith is not the holding of correct doctrines, but personal
fellowship with the living God. Correct doctrines will both

express this, and assist it and issue from it; incorrect doctrine will misrepresent this and hinder and prevent this." [4]
Faith involves a willingness to live in creaturely dependence
upon the promise of God instead of insisting upon a doctrine
for guaranteed living.

To clarify our point, let us listen to a man who explains
what faith means to him and what he is looking for.

" I feel I have to have some ideas I can believe with full
assurance regardless what happens." When we ask for
further explanation, he is able to spell out the content of
his faith with some precision as he understands it. " I believe that there is a God and that he is all-powerful and all-
loving. I believe that Jesus was his Son who preached,
taught, and worked miracles; that he died and rose again,
and his Spirit lives with us. I believe that man is essentially
good, that evil can be corrected, and the church can help.
I also believe there is a future life, especially for those who
have tried to live according to God's laws."

At this point, we are not concerned about *what* this man
believes, although what a person believes is of crucial importance to his life. Rather, we are concerned with *how* he
arrived at this conception of faith.

This young man, along with many others, is certain that
nothing will destroy what he has so carefully arranged as
" right," " correct," and "true." He understands faith as a
search for personal certitude and security. This does not
mean that we ignore or belittle " rigid belief," for the Christian faith requires right intellectual interpretations of the
gospel. But the point we want to make is that he is more
concerned with what truths he should accept in order to
have hope and peace of mind than with the God in whom
he should completely trust. As Luther says, " Faith does not
require information, knowledge, or security, but a free surrender and joyful daring upon an unfelt, untried, unknown
goodness." [5] Thus the problem is not what people prefer to
believe, but always wherein their actual trust lies. They

forget that faith is man's total surrender of the self to God's grace in Jesus Christ, and that this is more than " believing " in certain propositions and ideas.

There are those who think faith means knowing about something and that it should be preceded by a positive or objective knowledge of some particular truth about God or by some system of ideas and facts. In other words, they hold the common view that knowledge comes first and faith comes afterward.

A group of laymen who did not want to accept the traditional creeds of the church because they thought that they were too archaic and outmoded for the modern man asked the author to write a statement of faith for them. They wanted something that would give them an " idea " of what they should know before they could be convinced of the reality to which they should commit themselves or in other words " of what we are getting into."

" Tell me what to believe " is a common plea among our laymen. They want someone to give them, quickly and skillfully in a capsule form, a " faith " that is certified as being true and reliable. They would rather believe in certain ideas as true and acceptable by the church than experience the tension between the mercy of God on one hand and the sin of man on the other. They ask to be spared from the agony of struggle and despair. " I can't bear this agony and doubt anymore. I want someone to tell me what I should believe." These people have some understanding of the struggle of the venture of trust in God and are afraid to dig deep into their own existence and be found of God himself.

" I hear so many conflicting views that I am confused. I wish someone would tell me what the best view is. I think Roman Catholics are better off. They are told which is right and what they should believe," says a worried mother. How easy it is for an adult to slip from trusting God into trusting the clergyman, a professor, or the church, without realizing that they must still come to personal decision before God.

THE PROBLEM OF FAITH AND LEGALISM

One factor that rises to predominant importance for our consideration is the stubborn barrier of legalism or moralism. We have already made some general remarks on this subject; however, it is important to know that most adults, in some way or another, deep down are legalists in thought and action. They escape the reality of sin to find refuge in easy and superficial standards that they have set up and can measure up to without much effort.

They consider sin as man's willful violation of the law and define it in terms of petty sins to be avoided; they consider obedience to God as conformity to a prescribed code of regulations without regard to consequences. This concept of God represents a Pharisaic or moralistic sanction of their aspirations.

They are convinced that no change is required in motives and attitudes, and believe it is ridiculous that man should experience guilt. " Why should I feel guilty when I try my best to do what the Bible tells me to do? " " I don't have to feel guilty."

They misinterpret the Bible as a book of laws that are to be rigidly obeyed. They take pride in their good works, in their true knowledge of good and bad, in their faithfulness to the will of God as revealed in the teachings of the Bible.

Such an understanding degenerates into a barren observance of external actions and nearly always to Pharisaism and hypocrisy. Such people ignore man's finitude and sin and are unwilling to confess their lack of faith in God's redeeming power, and do not even care to think that repentance is possible. " I go to church, I pay my dues, I pray, I try to help others whenever there is a need. I'm happy." " We [husband and wife] do everything a Christian should do. The minister should be thankful that we are able to make it to church so often. We live such a distance." " As

far as religion is concerned, we are all right, thank God. We
do all that's necessary for being a church member."

In this connection it should be remembered that many
laymen justify themselves by " good works." They feel that
they have failed and must atone by doing something extra
for the church. " I feel so guilty for not knowing my faith,
so the best thing I can do is to teach Sunday school "! " I
feel so awful for not having attended church regularly that
all I can do is to raise my pledge." " I decided to give a
special gift to the building fund; I'm afraid I haven't been
a good church member." Clearly, these individuals have little
or no understanding of the doctrine of justification by faith.
They have little realization that the way to faith is not
through works but through repentance and acceptance of
God's grace in Jesus Christ.

The Problem of Faith and Idolatry

It is evident that Christians of our age are confronted by
the massive opposition of materialism and that we are engaged in a war of loyalties and ideologies. As we listen to
them, it becomes distressingly plain that they give their
loyalty to a wide assortment of gods even though they deny
them lip service, reserving this, presumably, for God. The
degree and the quality of the worship of idols is reflected in
the following illustrations as reported by laymen.

" My twelve-year-old son means everything to me, and I
can't live without him. Is this wrong? " asks an anxious
mother. Here is another woman who puts all her trust in
her home and family. " I have a good husband, three lovely
children, a nice home, and a steady income. That's all I
want," says she. A young man literally worships his long-
awaited child. " She means everything to me," he says. " I
can't live without her! Everything else is secondary in my
life. Does it mean I love her more than I love God? " An
intelligent lawyer trusts the goodness of his culture. " I have
a nice home, a cottage, a boat, two cars, and all the con-

veniences of modern life. Life is getting better and better, and this is what we should look for. After all, God wants us to live happily and without care! "

A young executive lives for the sake of his new home. He designs every detail of it, works on it in all his free hours, takes pride in his handicraft, and rejoices over his skill. As a result, he is unable to fulfill his responsibilities as the superintendent of the church school, but he wants to attend a study group because it gives him something different to do! A man who is used to holding offices in different organizations makes it very clear that he would not join the church if he is not made a deacon (he was made one!). A young man reports that he spends almost all his free time taking care of his car. He washes and polishes it practically every day. He keeps it in a garage, covered with a blanket, and uses it only when it is absolutely necessary! " Is this wrong? " he asks.

If this testimony and experience of adults (even if it sounds superficial to us) means anything at all, it amounts to the fact that there is, as Calvin said, a perfect factory of idols that claim their loyalty and trust. These are the idols of money, prestige, power, success, pleasure, leisure, reason, sex, position, church buildings, various expressions of do-goodism, democracies, ideologies, on which people depend for some security or foothold. We are often reminded of Martin Luther's comment that what you hang your heart on and confide in is your god. Many people " hang their hearts " on and confide in some idol of their own making, and the tragedy is that most of them do not know it!

A great number of adults are devotees of " inspirational literature " of " peace of mind," and of " positive thinking." The lady who says she reads from " inspirational " literature every night before she goes to bed and is interested in " successful living " is too timid to face the difficulties that the Christain faith presents to her thinking. People find comfort in flimsy substitutes and sentimental

ideas about God and his relation to the world. God is just
about all the good things that we are. " He has been good
to me. I have no complaints," says a self-satisfied man.
Identification of God with the interests and values of our
nation is common. " God is on our side. After all, we are
for him. Our nation was founded on belief in God," argues
an " old-timer." " How can we show to the world that our
way is better than the way of communism? " People often
talk too glibly and easily about God. " Deep down, I know
I believe in God. It's sort of like conscience telling you
what is right and wrong," one person explains.

Among the many beliefs that adults hold about God there
are fumbling, weird, and anthropomorphic ideas that have
domesticated God in such a way that he fades and is not
recognizable anymore. Some retain childish and meager ideas
of God as a benevolent man, a kindly, sweet, and loving
person, while others imagine him a vague, remote, and com-
paratively harmless person. For some the word " God " is
just another word, and for others it stands as one of those
overused words that have lost their meaning. In the minds
of people there is a wide gap between God as a " cosmic
pal " or " the man upstairs," and God as the " consuming
fire " of the letter to the Hebrews.

For some, God is so " remote " and so " near " at the
same time that it makes no difference whether he exists or
not. " I never thought of that before," says one. " What does
God have to do with politics? " asks a puzzled layman.
Often God serves as an emotional outlet and nothing else.
" The appearance of ' In God We Trust ' on our coins is the
best thing that could have happened to this country. It will
always remind people that this country is founded on faith
in God," explains another. The alarming fact about the
present human situation is that man's relation to the God
of Jesus Christ is not any better than that of Gogo and Didi
to Godot in *Waiting for Godot,* by Beckett. Such being the
religious orientation of the Protestant laymen, it is not our

prising that the God who is the object of such faith cannot claim their utter loyalty. We are reminded of Kierkegaard's words:

> The most dreadful sort of blasphemy is that of which Christendom is guilty: transforming the God of Spirit into . . . ludicrous twaddle. And the stupidest divine worship, more stupid than anything that is or was to be found in paganism, more stupid than worshiping a stone, an ox, an insect, more stupid than all that is — to worship under the name of God . . . a twaddler.[6]

All this is by way of pointing out that man believes whatever suits his fancy or fits his immediate motives. He feels free to choose his idols. He may pledge his loyalty when and where he pleases. In other words, man is engaged in what the Bible means by " idolatry." He has his way blocked by a variety of idols, all of which claim to be " true " faith.

From the above discussion we may conclude the following. First, it is quite clear that men are in need of some ultimate object of loyalty. They realize that they have to put their trust in something in order to live at all. Secondly, it becomes more and more obvious that there is a longing for release from the inner contradictions caused by a divided loyalty to these false gods. Men realize that they have a choice of masters, but they are unaware of the fact that any choice they make except God is disastrous, for no other god except the God of our Lord Jesus Christ can give them their true freedom. Deep down, they are also aware of the fact that these false gods are unable to save them from the frustrations of life, that no one of these can give continuous meaning to life, that they are not trustworthy — false gods die, fade away, or are replaced by others. But few realize that when these gods fail us, we shall be confronted with the choice between God and complete meaninglessness.

The natural questions, then, arise: If man lives by some faith relation and is in need of some ultimate object of loyalty, why does acknowledgment of the sovereignty of God

come hard? If he longs for meaning in life, why does he turn
away from the gospel?

The Problem of Faith and Reason

For many laymen, the conflict of faith and reason remains
the greatest intellectual barrier to an understanding of the
Christian faith. Although the struggle is not easily described,
it is very real and very obvious. People often admit the fact
that they live in a climate that is unfavorable to religious
faith and find themselves faced with an unbridged gulf between faith and reason.

As we have already stated, many still tend to define faith
in terms of passive acceptance of a set of rules. Others asso-
ciate faith with blind submission to some creed. Reason, on
the other hand, they tend to regard as the only way to truth.
In other words, if something lies beyond the conclusions of
sense perception so that it cannot be proved and scientifically
verified, the verdict is that it is improbable and incredible,
and therefore it should be abandoned. Some go so far as to
see nothing but the world of the test tube and the IBM com-
puter. When people accept scientific criteria as the sole
method of ascertaining truth, we should not be surprised to
find so many agnostics.

Although the majority of people who attend a study group
are neither scientists nor sophisticated intellectuals, the prestige of science has been so great and its influence has spread
so widely that scientific habits have gradually influenced the
thinking of average Christians. Many assume, consciously
and unconsciously, that scientific knowledge is the source of
rational belief. They believe that faith can be proven by rational demonstrations. They use some sweeping assumptions
to show what could and what could not happen. Many are so
obsessed with the pseudoscientific view of a closed universe
that they present argument instead of fact to deny the rea-
sonableness of faith. But the problem is that they stop here
and are not concerned with the unique and the "unlikely,"

which is the basis of theoretical science as well as of religious faith.

Those who hold the scientific viewpoint expect to be argued into faith by empirical evidence. A couple who had witnessed the healings at Lourdes insisted that this experience changed their lives and for the first time they realized that faith in God is possible. People like these hold an empirical conception of truth, namely, whatever cannot be proved empirically or lies outside the realm of natural experience is either not quite true or not quite certain.

There are also adults who search for truth insofar as truth can be discovered by reason, concepts, and logic. As an illustration, let us consider the case of an intelligent and well-read philosophy major, a church member, a deacon, who attended the study group quite regularly for a period of three months. During the discussions he baldly and honestly demanded intelligibility and comprehensiveness; he challenged the logic of theological language; he argued in favor of the superiority of reason over faith; he used philosophical arguments and analogies to prove the unreasonableness of the Christian faith, and pointed to the lack of convincing logic in supporting the statements of faith. At times he would feel uncertain of the truth of his basic philosophy, but his feelings could not stand up against the critique of his intellect and he was unwilling to question the validity of his reason. He was doubtful whether Pascal and Kierkegaard were right in trying to convince modern skeptics that when mathematical certainty is unattainable " the leap " into belief should be dared. After all, he would argue, faith cannot be enforced by any willed effort or intentional decision; moreover, no objective truth can ever be found on the merely subjective truthfulness of the believer.

Throughout our discussion it was apparent that he was more interested in establishing himself as a man of independent thought than in discovering the truth. From time to time he would admit that he had genuine intellectual difficulties about the Christian faith. But he could not deny that the question of God, seen from a merely theoretical point of view, constituted a fundamental problem. Besides, he could not ignore the significance of the idea of the covenant God for the Christian community. Further, he was always impressed by the fact that throughout the centuries there have been people of vital faith, not in the God of the philosophers, but in the God of Abraham, Jacob, Isaac, and of our Lord Jesus Christ.

At the end of the course our friend made the following statement to the author: " You ministers and teachers of religion should not take the problem of faith and reason too seriously. Some arrive at an understanding of God through reason or theoretical knowledge; others like myself realize that they have a long battle to fight, and still others hope for the moment when what you call revelation will come as a flash of insight, then we shall understand."

It's true that this particular case reflects the condition of the intellectual elite, but we can also say that this is only one example from among many which show the intellectual depth of some of our adults and the conflict between reason and faith as a barrier to faith. Some may say our friend was not quite honest enough to face the truth about himself; others would think he evaded it through an escape into intellectual discourse, and still others would argue that he was not willing to admit his true and vital need. Whatever the case, here was a person like many others, who was quite close to an understanding of the Christian faith as a spectator who stands aloof, but unwilling to stand in the crisis of commitment and hesitant to place himself existentially inside the circle of the believing community and let his faith be tested by the self-validating experience of communion with God, in Christ in the fellowship of the believers.

In still another area there are the endlessly fascinating and perplexing questions of the origin and validity of knowledge. " How do we know that we know? " " Can religious knowledge be reliable? " " How can we know whether Christ or Mohammed or Buddha has experienced an authentic revelation? " " How can one tell an ' authentic religious experience ' from superstitious nonsense? " " Maybe reported experiences of God are merely experiences within the minds of men. How can we tell? " These are among those questions which deal with the problem of knowledge and arouse a good deal of disturbance. In other words, adults challenge us to prove that faith has a rational foundation. They ask for evidence that belongs to rational knowledge instead of the knowledge of faith.

In a less sophisticated way adults argue the fact that there are many levels of knowledge and that because the world is so vast and so complex, we need to employ a rich variety of means of knowledge. They tell us how wrong the church is when it dogmatizes about what man can and cannot know. " How do you know there are no angels? " one man asks. " I cannot confidently say or believe that there are no angels, although I have never seen one," he argues. " After all, isn't it safer to sit on the saddle rather loosely when it comes to the problem of knowing? " adds another.

" Since I cannot know everything for sure, why bother? " " Why should I make up my mind now what I believe and what I don't believe? I'll wait until man gains more knowledge and comes closer to truth." " I know there is no such thing as perfect knowledge, so I'm not too fanatic about whether Christianity is the truest religion or not."

On the one hand, these statements are disturbing; on the other hand, such an attitude becomes even more disturbing when these adults show no concern about the impossibility of knowledge. Thus, the problem of knowledge remains a barrier to faith.

The Problem of Faith and Doubt

The conflict of belief and disbelief, of faith and doubt, has always been a serious problem in the life of the believers. We are told that in our day a trend toward a new kind of religious skepticism is clearly discernible. It is argued that the modern skeptic longs despairingly for some kind of faith to fill the void created by the death of old gods. Disillusioned with progress and having lost faith in man-made replicas, he has a terrible longing to believe.[7] We may also add that this kind of skepticism has been encouraged and intensified by man's expanding knowledge and experience as well as by the church's failure in recognizing that doubt and faith be viewed as the expression of man's two most basic needs.

Since doubt hides behind certain masks and appears under special conditions, it is necessary to reveal its true nature. When a layman says, " I'm skeptical " or " I'm doubtful " about this or that, exactly what does he mean? What is he doubting? To what is he reacting? What is he rejecting, and on what ground?

Although the problem of doubt is personal and as varied in significance as is personality itself, there are certain modes of doubt that are especially common among the adults. In the following pages we shall attempt to discuss how adults express their doubts and what these doubts reveal about their religious faith. Some of these expressions may sound naïve and show lack of intelligent understanding of the Christian faith; however, since laymen take them seriously, we too should consider them important and remember that doubt is not always a negation of faith but is a position that represents a religious faith characterized by pertinent questioning rather than by affirmation.

Intellectual Doubt

In the previous pages we have shown how adults reveal their doubts through the questions they ask. We have also pointed out the conflict between reason and faith that is often a denial of the possibility of a knowledge that transcends rational knowledge, and hence a barrier to faith.

Brunner believes that doubt is the intellectual form of sin, he says:

> Doubt is not a function of the reason as such, but it is the fruit of the falsely autonomous human reason, which sets itself up as an absolute authority. It does not spring from intellectual honesty, but from intellectual arrogance. It springs from the erroneous and sinful fundamental axiom that human reason is the measure of all things, that everything that lays claim to truth must prove itself before the court of rational argument. This declaration of sovereignty and autonomy by the human reason is simply the desire to be like God, or self-deification.[8]

The foregoing discussion is self-explanatory. Modern man refuses to take God seriously; as Calvin said, it is " the sinful effort to put God out of mind." Man has such a great confidence in the self-sufficiency of human reason that he finds it difficult to rely on the sovereignty of God lest it impede the free exercise of the mind.

We now turn our attention to those who say, " I want to believe *but* I can't believe because I'm afraid I won't agree with what the Bible says." " Will it work if I believe? " Some are afraid that most of the Christian beliefs cannot be justified rationally or scientifically. Many laymen are quite frank in expressing their doubts by challenging those statements which, if taken literally, would offend the common sense. They reveal the depth of their rebellion against any idea which in their opinion insults the common sense and seems repressive to intelligence. " The reason why I did not join the church is that I could not swallow the Apostles' Creed. I couldn't even bear reading it on Sundays." In this scientific age, they claim, the miracles, the virgin birth, and the resurrection are no longer intelligible to the modern mind. On one hand, these people are engaged in scientific discussion; on the other hand, they are not willing to widen their categories of truth and validity and face the fact that these " miracles " may be intelligible in some other way because they are afraid that even such explanations cannot be justified rationally. This is the most vicious of all vicious circles, which threatens one's faith and creates a serious crisis of doubt.

A further observation that is worth mentioning and is closely connected with what has already been said is the case of those who are anxiously searching for certainty, yet plagued with the threat that such a search is in vain. We are thinking of a medical research person who says: " I want to be both a Christian and a scientist, but I'm afraid it can never be done. The two are incompatible." If he considers his laboratory and the altar both belonging to the same world, he thinks that there is little hope for intellectual integrity. Let us not forget that intellectual obstacles to faith are the result of the intellectual element in the Christian faith itself, but when the intellect becomes autonomous, then the very meaning of life is at stake.

" The Scandal of Particularity "

One of the most serious obstacles to faith is the challenge of the exclusiveness of Christianity and its evangelical claim that is the basis of the motive of missions. In other words, the " scandal of particularity " is a stumbling block; it is offensive and incredible to many Protestant laymen. This has become not only an intellectual problem but an existential one.

Because of the increasing knowledge of anthropology, various interpretations of the origin of cultures and religions, the influence of Zen Buddhism in some circles, and the contact of Christians with people of other faiths, especially in Asian countries, laymen have come to the point not only of challenging the exclusiveness of Christianity but of arguing for the validity of other faiths.

How can Christianity claim uniqueness when religions are so similar and when their origins are social? How can Christianity claim to have a monopoly of all truth when there is some truth in all religions? " One religion is as good as the other "; or, " All religions are equally though differently true." The popular notion that there are many ways — just as there are paths on different sides of a mountain all pointing to the top and all succeeding in reaching the top — is well known to many. They claim that all religions are merely varied expressions of the same truths that people of all ages and cultures held. " I'm so happy that my daughter married a Moslem fellow! " says a mother proudly. " What difference does it make? He believes in the same God as we do." " We have a lot to learn from other faiths," adds someone. " For instance, why do we frown at the Hindu idea of the reincarnation? Doesn't it have to do with immortality? It really makes sense! "

Sometimes this is a kind of indifference that would be fatally destructive if it were applied to science. They find it difficult to realize that a religious neutralism can become destructive when it fails to distinguish between the more true and the less true.

There is what one may call a kind of syncretism that has little to do with the Biblical faith. People try hard to reconcile conflicting ideas. Some are of the belief, as we have already seen, that it makes no difference what kind of faith a person has as long as he believes in God (who need not be the God of Jesus Christ).

The famous saying of Hendrik Kraemer that the " church is mission " means very little to many laymen. It's interesting to discover that American Protestants feel more justified in " converting " the next-door neighbor, who claims he has no religion, to Christianity, than a Muslim or a Buddhist who lives in some corner of the world. There is a false assumption that Christians have something of their own to give to others. " How can I tell a Hindu that my religion is better than his when I know I'm not a better person than he is? " asks a worried schoolteacher. Their justification for the motive of mission is a vague goodness or a religious view, and

usually their conviction that we need to have fraternal workers to teach, heal, and even preach, is part of that being good
or being helpful to others less fortunate and the unprivileged.
Such an attitude provides a base for a vague theological syncretism. It saves them from the "scandal of particularity,"
and institutional identification with the West.

The foregoing discussion fits well with the virtue of tolerance or the spirit of brotherhood that many people are so
proud of. Here is an adult who is eager to please everybody
because there is no use, he thinks, in hurting other people's
feelings. " Everybody has his own religion and his own point
of view," he says, " and I have no right to claim that my
idea is better than the others'. " " This is true," adds another.
" There must always be two sides to every question. I hope
I can teach that to my children." " Our problem is that we
are not tolerant enough of each other's beliefs," says another.

These statements make sense and are worthy of praise as
they stand. However, such a tolerance is neither in the name
of " brotherliness of toleration " nor in the name of a quest
for truth. Some of these people are too " humble " and too
" tolerant " to accept or to deserve what has been offered to
them in Jesus Christ.

> " I don't know why I should be the person who deserves
> all the favor! "
> " It's not your fault — you were born in it, and why not
> just accept it and make the best of it? "
> " Yes, that makes the problem even more serious and
> that's why the least I can do is to be humble about it, to
> the point that if need be, I can accept other people's point
> of view and even their religious truths."

This kind of self-defensive humility is another way of saying that a person does not need Christ because he does not
deserve him. Such humility is deeply rooted in man's perennial problem of pride. He is too stubborn to wake to the full

seriousness of his own guilt and of his own inability to overcome it, and too proud to receive God's love and forgiveness in Jesus Christ.

It may not be without significance also to mention the fact that sometimes there is a confusion between the problem of toleration and the question of truth. There are those who are " tolerant," yet at the same time they do not believe that there is truth in another person's ideas. " When I question my own religion, I don't mean to say that other religions are correct. As a matter of fact, I doubt everything they say." A similar point is made by another adult who says: " The whole thing is just a big talk. A Hindu is as wrong as I am and as true in his ideas as I, so we cancel each other."

This kind of " toleration " is a refusal to be aware of the depth of the human problem, and the rejection of the fact that both Hindu and Christian alike need God's redemption and forgiving love. It is another way of saying, " I know I'm wrong, but I don't feel guilty enough to want help."

Doubt and Rebellion

Laymen express their doubt as rebellion, the roots of which are firmly planted in pride and self-sufficiency. They turn all of their attention upon themselves and are unwilling to look elsewhere.

Here is someone who, as Luther said, is " curved in upon himself." He evades every issue that he thinks will make him change his mind because he is convinced that he can never be wrong. He is among those who hide behind the old idea that one cannot teach an old dog new tricks, an idea that is still common and carries with it sufficient weight to block thinking and believing. Such a person withdraws or gets angry, and sometimes argues heatedly to protect his tightly held beliefs and opinions. He believes so fanatically that he looks for only those answers which would leave him unchanged and thus dominant over them, rather than receptive to them. At the end of a twelve weeks' course, an adult made the comment that he was glad nobody could change his mind. " I know I'm always right," he said with great pride. Here is one who is the master of his fate, captain of his soul, but given to pride and self-sufficiency.

Another example is the individual who shows self-will and arrogance. " It is sheer nonsense," he says, " to think that man cannot truly understand the mystery of himself except as God gives him this possibility. I teach psychology and I know that it is not true." The problem in this case is not the conflict between two points of view. It is a problem of the attitude this person holds. He thinks that because he teaches psychology, he can never be wrong. Our experience with such persons can be multiplied many times and we realize that as long as they hold on to their own point of view tightly the conflict remains unresolved. We realize that the problem is not simply unbelief, but as Barth says, " hate of the truth."

A further demonstration that unmasks the nature of doubt is seen when a person rejects that which attacks his fondly cherished ideas and the attitudes that have kept the image of himself safe and comfortable in the world around him. In order to protect the security of his present position he rejects that which threatens to shatter his loyalty to his self, which has become a prisoner of antiquity and self-complacency.

I am reminded of a young executive who, after attending a few sessions, called me to give his reasons for not wanting to continue to attend the study group. He said: " To be honest, I don't see why I should believe what others tell me. After all, I have my own opinion as to what is right and wrong. Besides, it's too late for me to change my mind. Making new decisions is a painful and harmful business. I'm satisfied with what I already know; maybe they are old-fashioned beliefs, but they're all right." Sometimes such people take strong dogmatic positions on issues, and express opinions unambiguously in black-and-white terms in order to maintain intellectual and spiritual nonconformity.

It remains now to call attention to one further example,

namely, the person who hides behind the quest for truth and considers his doubt as intellectual honesty. A member of a study group claims that he is going through intellectual turmoil as to whether he should join the church or not. Actually, he is trying to find reasons to justify his present feelings and opinions in order to avoid a commitment that would change his present attitude and behavior. " In all honesty, I can't bring myself to join the church. Intellectually, its teachings don't appeal to me, and besides, church members are not better people than those outside the church." He is determined that whatever answer he receives must be acceptable to his already held views. Here is the obstinacy of the mind as well as of the heart. Man cannot hear an answer because in the depth of his being he has already rejected it.

To summarize briefly, we call attention to the fact that there are willful, stubborn, and rebellious people who will *not* change for the simple reason that they do not need the faith. They reflect man's unwillingness to accept his situation as a dependent person, and his effort to free himself from the threats of insecurity by his own power of freedom, finding it impossible to trust the grace of God.

Doubt and Submission

It is not unusual to meet people who have never quite known what to think or believe. They swing from one position to the next, and are never satisfied with anything because they doubt everything. " I don't know what I should believe." " Sometimes I wonder if I believe anything." Some of these adults attend all types of study groups and every time they talk they express a new belief. " Everything I hear and learn is so good and so interesting that I don't want to make up my mind what I should believe." Or, " I learn all kinds of answers to my questions, so I don't have to worry about making decisions as to where I stand."

An idle wanderer moves from one idea to another out of sheer irresoluteness and under the guise of a quest for truth.

" I'll keep on searching until I find the right answer," he says. " It's too early now to make up my mind." Or, " It's good to hear all sides first, and then I'll make up my mind."

These people have no real comprehension of the importance of the Christian faith, nor are they willing to think deeply enough to realize the seriousness of life. They refuse to accept the fact that life has its tragedies, disillusionments, and frustrations; they are not in the mood to consider the cross as a stumbling block; they cannot bear the tragic answer to " Why did Jesus die? " In short, they make an attempt to deny that they are set over against the mercy and love of God; they prefer to feel that life is gay, carefree, and happy.

Doubt and Inadequate Ideas

Faulty understanding in addition to careless thinking leads many adults to doubt the validity of the Christian faith. " I don't believe in prayer anymore. I prayed day and night, but God did not spare my brother's life." " I always believed that being a Christian means being free from anxiety and care, but I have discovered in my own experience that this is not true, and I'm afraid as a result my faith has become quite shaky," says a worried adult.

Corruption of Christianity, in addition to false information or ignorance of the truths of the Christian faith gives rise to skepticism. " If that's what the Bible teaches [supremacy of the white race], I'm afraid I don't want to be called Christian! " says he bravely. " One of the reasons why I kept away from the church for a long time and doubted whether the Christian faith makes any sense or not was because I was told that Christianity puts more emphasis on the future life and has little to do with life in this world, except telling people to be nice."

Many think that they deny certain concepts of the Christian faith, but what they are denying are false concepts or mistaken notions, and they are right in rejecting them. For instance one person says, " I don't believe in the Trinity, because I don't believe that there are three Gods."

Pseudopsychology pushes people toward the perils of cheap rationalization and mental tricks. Some argue, for instance, that man's inventive faculty enters into his religious ideas. A woman who had lost her only son in a plane crash once said: " I used to believe in life after death, but since my son's death I realize that most of our hopes are just wishful thinking. I don't believe anymore that there is a future life! "

One detects a hidden pride in the statement of a schoolteacher who says, " If we can never know God and if he still remains a mystery, then what we say about him is just a fantasy and human inventions of metaphors and images." To prove the point, someone else comments: " Even the Old Testament itself says that throughout centuries man has changed his concept of God. Doesn't this mean that man's ideas about God change according to his situation? Aren't we really imagining things about God? "

Unreflective faith accepted mainly on authority or based on the dogmatism of an earlier training stimulates rebellion and leads to doubt. " All my life I was taught what to believe and was forced to accept the fact that what I was told was the only truth. Now I have come to the point that I don't believe anything! " says a worried young mother. Such a doubt proves to be of great value, for she has come to realize that what she already has was never her own and must be replaced by her own genuine personal belief.

Sometimes skepticism is actually a reaction to the traditional teachings of the church that have become authoritative, and it substitutes for vital faith; at other times skepticism results from a clash between the old and the new. Some express their doubts when they find that newly discovered ideas clash with previously accepted beliefs. New ideas startle them and often scare them because their old cherished ideas are thus placed under a cloud of doubt and suspicion.

" I always believed in immortality; now I'm all confused in trying to understand the difference between immortality and resurrection." " I have always believed — way back — in angels, but now I don't, and it's awfully disturbing." " I used to think Jesus was God; now I'm all confused! " Sometimes such a conflict becomes so dramatic that the person thinks he has lost his faith and decides to terminate once and for all his quest for religious meaning.

What shall we say about the literal-minded person for whom certain ideas have been frozen into fixed positions, and who is encouraged to reflect upon meanings, to distinguish between probable fact and myth, and to separate superstitions from reality? In such cases confusion with consequent doubt is bound to arise. He has lived with answers that presuppose no questions for such a long time that any insecurity belonging to faith threatens his cozy world. Moving from unyielding certitude to willingness to be open is very costly because there is so much that is frightening, and it is so consoling to be closed.

Faith and Doubt

Adults who are believing and conscientious know that they are caught between the tension of faith and doubt, and so they suffer agonies of disbelief. They are aware of an internal struggle that causes anxiety over what they call " loss of faith." They worry about their perplexity, which raises the question, " What does it mean ' God loves me '? " or " Does it really matter what I believe, after all? " " The more I think I trust God, the more I become aware of my doubts, and it scares me no end," says a layman anxiously.

The painful uncertainty that is the challenging nature of faith does, to a certain extent, account for the inevitable doubt. People become quite upset when they realize that in many areas of life a complete answer is not only impossible but also dangerous. But what upsets them most is why this uncertainty should lead them to doubt. Take, for instance, the perennial problem of evil and suffering as discussed in the previous chapter. Some are particularly disturbed when they are warned of the lack of certainty. " I get so upset when I realize I'll never know God." " I try so hard to know God's will and the harder I try, the more desperate I get! " Many feel guilty in expressing doubt about the message that God in Jesus Christ participates in human history and suffering. " How is this possible — it couldn't be! " or " How is Jesus also the Christ? "

Often, death produces doubt. " How can I believe there is meaning in life when death puts an end to everything? " " Is life really meaningful? " " How can I tell? " " It is hard to believe in future life when it is only a promise."

This kind of doubt is what Tillich calls existential doubt, which " does not question whether a special proposition is true or false. It does not reject every concrete truth, but it is aware of the element of insecurity in every existential truth." [9] He goes on to say, "Existential doubt and faith are poles of the same reality," and that " serious doubt is confirmation of faith." [10]

A person who expresses his honest doubts and suffers the agonies of disbelief accepts his finitude, and is closer to truth than one who lives with unruffled affirmations of faith. He should be helped to understand that such doubt is not " total doubt," as Tillich calls it. Rather, it is a quest for truth that may open new meanings and new ways of understanding. Aulén says, " Trust itself includes a trembling, which does not cease during this life, because man is man and God is God." [11] Thus, he who believes, believes also as an unbeliever, for only the sinner can be justified, and he who doubts, doubts also as a man of faith, for only the justified is the justified sinner.

◇ III ◇

A PURPOSE FOR CHRISTIAN
ADULT EDUCATION

If the attempt of the preceding chapters has been successful, two things should now be evident: First, laymen long for a life of faith with God although such faith comes hard. Second, in quest of truth and meaning, they find themselves involved in some kind of dialectical method of question and answer, of faith and doubt.

What we must consider now is a purpose or a goal for Christian adult education that will be more than an epilogue to what has already been said by Christian educators. To be sure, we have already anticipated our purpose by indicating that man's most serious need is a transcendent faith that will liberate him from his anxiety of distrust and skepticism. Still, what remains to be done is to discuss the implications of the purpose of Christian adult education.

Lewis Sherrill defines Christian education in such terms as these: " Christian education is the attempt, ordinarily by members of the Christian community, to participate in and to guide the changes which take place in persons in their relationships with God, with the church, with other persons, with the physical world, and with oneself." [12]

We note that for Sherrill, the purpose of Christian education is to give guidance to the changes that personalities undergo in relationships. This " change " or " new " relationship is the result of man's understanding of the self and of the world as he responds to God's revelation in Jesus Christ.

Sherrill believes that through this encounter with God, man comes to know certain things about himself as a self, about his relations in depth, or with another, and about his relationship to ultimate reality.

A further observation that cautions us against a traditional definition of Christian education is made by John Fry: " Christian education proceeds toward the enlargement of thinking. It finds, with all education, that its chief allies are plain ordinary curiosity and extraordinary imagination. Its foes, too, are the same, to wit: reaction, prejudice, disinterest, and fanaticism. Christian education seeks not to give or to help or to save or to convert, but to teach the thinking man to think." [13]

Fry puts the emphasis on *thinking,* but a different kind of thinking and occasionally with a different kind of result. He defines thinking as a " charismatic event " for the man of faith, and considers it as the only distinction and the glory of Christian education. He believes that this kind of thinking is uniquely Christian, because it is " faithful thinking " in the sense that faith meditates upon itself and its own content.[14]

For our purpose, it may not be without significance to quote a definition of general education by Philip H. Phenix, professor of education, Teachers College, Columbia. He says: " The central task of education is religious conversion. This is not to be understood in the conventional sense, as securing commitment to a special organized church or acceptance of one of the traditional creeds. What is meant is the *inner transformation of purpose and motive from self-regarding irreligious and the idolatrous service of limited goals to reverent service of the Most High.*"[15] (Italics are mine.)

Education as an inner transformation of purpose and motive, and as the redirecting of life from finite attachment to the ultimate commitment, is an exciting challenge. Phenix points out that to accomplish this change is the supreme end of all teaching and learning.

In common with these three thinkers, we take the position that Christian education can and should assist the adult to think — to think charismatically, and to guide the conversion experiences that take place in an encounter with God, and hence with the self, with others, and with the world. If, for the sake of argument, we had to synthesize these positions, we would say: The function of Christian adult education is *to guide the converted man to think charismatically.* However, since the word " conversion " suggests an abrupt change, we prefer to say, *the sovereign test of Christian education of adults is whether or not it tends to lead the adults toward the inexplicable change of mind called repentance.*

What is repentance and how do we define education? " Repentance " is an old-fashioned word that is usually known, at least to the modern man, as a more or less pious subjective experience. We recall that Jesus made " Repent, and believe " (Mark 1:15) the keynote of his Galilean ministry and the requirement of entry into the Kingdom of God. The two words are closely related and should not be separated, for repentance means turning from sin, and faith means turning to God. The encounter with God in Jesus Christ produces both repentance and faith, and both are God's gift, and are not man's achievement. In other words, repentance involves the active acceptance of God's gift of faith,[16] " For by grace you have been saved through faith; and this is not your own doing, it is the gift of God " (Eph. 2:8).

Education, on the other hand, according to definition, means to learn, to gain knowledge or understanding by " a formal course of study, instruction, or training. So, what we want to say is that education — specifically the kind of education that gets its distinctive character from the Christian faith — can lead adults toward change of mind or repentance.

Having thus stated the view by which the Christian education of adults may be tested, we must look at the objections that are bound to rise. There is, first, the question of the position in which this view places Christian education. Does it not push nurture or education out of its proper place and toward preaching or evangelism? Secondly, how can we avoid trying to predetermine for others what they should be, and how can we resist the temptation to manipulate them to make the ends sought come true?

In the first place, since our problem of Christian education is the problem of how a person can be confronted by God who alone can bring about a change in him, and since this involves the problem of communication of the Christian message, it is necessary to arrive at an understanding of the Biblical concept of man and the nature of his faith. Secondly, we shall specify some functions of Christian adult education in terms of interpreting and witnessing the Christian faith. Meantime, we shall raise the big question whether or not it is possible within an educational process to reach the goal set before us.

Man and Faith

The Bible makes it clear that the glory of man is that he has been created in God's image in a covenant relationship with God. He bears from the beginning the image of God's will and purpose in his inmost self, and his uniqueness lies in the fact of his obligation to God, namely, to live in communion with him and in harmony with his fellowman.

But man is also God's creature. He is finite, he is created, he is not self-sufficient, he still hopes to become what he was supposed to be. Man is beloved of God, yet he stands under God's judgment because of his continual failure in his responsibility to his Creator. He is a sinner, alienated from God and his fellowman, and burdened by his guilt. Created with capacity to think, to purpose, and to love, man is unable of himself to enter into fellowship with God and hence live in harmony with his neighbor.

The two contradictory elements in man's life, namely, his being created in God's image and his creatureliness, or his glory and his misery, are reconciled through God's act in Jesus Christ. The Scriptures affirm that it is God's intent — therefore, the human possibility — that man enter into communion with God and grow up toward a realization of his destiny of becoming the child of God. This destiny of man can be fulfilled only by God's reconciling love in Jesus Christ. Through Christ, he is to be raised to God's image. God has come and continues to come, seeking man to draw him into communion with him by the offer of new life in Jesus Christ. This is God's covenant promise of faithfulness and his guarantee of his unconditional love to man.

But the fellowship of God and man, for which man was destined, demands a complete reorientation of the total self. The human possibility, in order to be realized, requires a genuine transformation of human concern from self-reliance to reliance upon God's grace, from fear to faith, from self-confidence to confidence born of a new understanding of self-acceptance under God's judgment and grace in Jesus Christ.

This complete reorientation of the entire personality, this shattering of spiritual and moral complacency, or *repentance* if you will, becomes a reality when God in Christ breaks through the human situation and reveals himself to man. In this encounter, as Brunner says, Christ reveals man to himself in his need before the righteous, majestic, yet loving God while revealing God before finite, sinful, yet hopefully striving man, as the ultimate object of his trust.[17] In other words, through Christ, God shows man to himself and at the same time reveals his judgment and grace. In this experience, man's response to God is that of faith and total commitment even when he fails to comprehend God with his mind. He experiences some new truths, new insight, new meaning, which lights up other truths. No single term adequately explains this new condition. Paul speaks of the " new creation " in Christ; Tillich refers to the " New Being." In spite of peripheral differences of thought, there is

an agreement that when man comes to the end of his limit
and is grasped by Christ he cannot help putting his ultimate
truth upon Him. How this takes place and how it can be
interpreted remains a prime theological concern for Christian education. The initiative and basic promptings come
from God to man, and man makes this gift his own. This
means that God does not and will not " save " a person
against his will.

In the life of faith, man comes to an understanding of
the Sovereign God who is Lord and with whom he can enter
into communion as creature before Creator. He finds his
ultimate dependence upon God who grasps him, gives himself in love and forgiveness, and redirects his life. Man
discovers that he is able to meet his daily tasks not by his
own effort, but by the power of God and in a continuous
surrender to him. Recognizing that he does not create the
energies by which he lives and realizing that the source of
life is in God who is the ground of being, man gratefully
accepts his existence as a gift from God. He realizes that
he cannot truly comprehend the mystery of himself save as
God gives him this possibility; he is aware of the fact that
he cannot find the meaning of life save as God gives him
the meaning.

The life of faith that is continuous encounter with God
and a process of growing up to the fullness of God's likeness
is never completed and is never perfect. As a matter of fact,
it remains under God's judgment. This change of mind, or
repentance, is not an experience that takes place once for
all. It is a continuous experience. As long as man lives in
the flesh he is never emancipated from all pride, idolatry,
guilt, anxiety, doubt, temptations, and self-assertion. He
realizes that his life of faith, his moral actions, and his intellectual tasks are tainted with self-interest and exploitation of others. He knows that he has left undone those things
which he ought to have done and he has done those things
which he ought not to have done. His life continues with

frustrations, restlessness, and abiding anxieties. This is because he has no power to overcome them, and he is always in danger of slipping back to self-centeredness in every situation in one way or another.

Further, the life of faith bears the mark of uncertainty, tentativeness, and apprehensiveness. It opens up the way toward a kind of maturity that is replete with crisis, struggle, uncertainties, conflict, and anxiety. Man finds himself summoned by God to live in readiness for new possibilities and duties as a free, thinking man. He realizes that God continually calls him to exert the full capacities of his freedom, to risk, to suffer, to make decisions and exercise his human gifts. But he is always haunted by the idea that he has not loved God with all his heart and soul, and all his mind and strength; he has not loved his neighbor as himself. He is aware of the fact that he has not exhausted all the possibilities of reconciliation in human relations; he has not done his best to eradicate social injustices, prejudice, and ignorance; he has not wholeheartedly fought indifference, lethargy, and laziness. He realizes that no matter how hard he tries to enter into relation of faith and love with God and man, there is more that could and ought to be done.

Thus man stands before the righteousness of God, which is made bearable only by God's gracious acceptance of man in Jesus Christ. He realizes that the possibility of forgiveness and the new life is always offered anew to him through the life, death, and resurrection of Jesus Christ, and he must live in constant repentance if he is to live at all before the righteous and gracious God.

Finally, the new life in faith is a life that is sustained by the consciousness of God's grace in Christ. Man realizes that God in Christ accepts him as he actually is — not the ideal self he wishes he were or the weak self he despises himself for being. God's acceptance of him is his true justification. He realizes not only that his life has been forgiven and is daily made new but also that his future is graced by God.

Thus, knowing himself accepted by God, he dares to accept others because they have been accepted by him too. Having been reconciled to God, he feels reconciled with all men through Christ. He lives his life hopefully toward an end that is, like our destinies themselves, in God's keeping. As Calvin says, " Truly, faith justifies us for no other reason than that it reconciles us to God, and this not by its own merit, but only because as we receive the grace offered to us in the promises and are certainly persuaded that we are loved by God as sons, we also come to possess the assurance of life eternal." [18]

Thus, the life of faith experiences God as Creator, who creates that man may enter into communion with him; as Judge, who judges in order to redeem; and as Redeemer, in order that man may live in continuous relationship of reconciliation and acceptance with God and his fellowmen. Furthermore, this life of faith is nourished by true communion with God. It worships God because nothing else is worthy of supreme devotion; for man's chief end is to glorify God and enjoy him forever.

It remains now to call attention to another phase of faith that has a direct bearing upon our thesis. This new life of faith includes a new understanding or knowledge that God reveals to man in his act of grace in Jesus Christ.

What is this knowledge? The word " knowledge " has various subtle meanings in the Bible. Generally, this concept of knowledge is not synonymous with intellectual achievement, academic understanding, or philosophical truth that has been learned. It is not merely the outcome of intuition, or the acquaintance with the Christian tradition, either. It may include all these, but it is more. It connotes a deeper level of understanding or perception that is beyond the individual's thought and will, and engages his total existence — his emotion, will, and action. It is a new kind of enlightenment that brings about a new way of life. Paul prays for the members of the community, that they " may be filled with the knowledge of his will in all spiritual wisdom and understanding " (Col. 1:9). In trying to express the unique nature of the believer's relation to Christ, the New Testament states that such relationship involves an element of knowledge,[19] and recognizes this knowledge as a gift of the Spirit: " To one is given through the Spirit the utterance of wisdom, and to another the utterance of knowledge according to the same Spirit " (I Cor. 12:8). It is a gift because no one can discover it for himself; it has been given to man by God's grace in Jesus Christ.

Thus, to have new knowledge does not mean to acquire a new philosophy of life, but to go through a transformation of the self, and surrender one's self to God in Jesus Christ for the direction of life. The person who goes through such an experience has already obeyed by making a decision, not because he has consciously willed, but because of something that has worked through him " despite himself." He has gone through a process of conversion.

To summarize our discussion so far, we shall make the following observations. First, we find that repentance is a continuous process but also a very human one that is available to everyone. Secondly, the dynamic nature of faith is a new kind of understanding in which man sees himself in relation to Christ and lives in a continuous surrender to him.

In the light of the foregoing discussion of man as a creature and yet created in God's image, and the nature of faith as man's reception of God's grace in Jesus Christ, the nature of Christian education of adults begins to be clarified, namely, to lead individuals to an understanding of themselves as beings created in God's image who live against their destiny, and yet heirs of God's grace in Jesus Christ.

Now we have to face the challenge whether such a purpose will ultimately lead the adult to repentance. How is it possible in an educational situation to come to a commitment of God in Jesus Christ for the direction of life? Paul says, " Faith comes from what is heard, and what is heard comes by the preaching of Christ." (Rom. 10:17.) Is it possible, then, in an educational situation to inculcate such faith or to lead laymen to such a radical decision in relation to God's grace that their whole existence is involved? Is not this the function of preaching rather than teaching? Bultmann says: " Education or training of the will is useless. What is needed is to bring home to the will its utter impotence: so that it can say: ' O wretched man that I am! Who shall deliver me from the body of this death? ' " [20] After all, traditionally, the purpose of Christian nurture is to instruct those who are already in the community in the meaning of the faith so that they may " grow in the grace and knowledge of our Lord Jesus Christ," and the function of preaching is to awaken faith, or to evangelize and to convert.

Before we venture into a detailed discussion of the issue before us, namely, the unique task of Christian education, the following points need to be considered seriously.

First, we should be aware of the oversimplification of the problem of believer and unbeliever. But who is a believer? According to the New Testament, a believer is a person who has been grasped and transformed by Jesus Christ. In the language of a layman, a believer is one who accepts what his church offers him as the truth of the Christian faith. It is easy to assume that those who attend study groups are all believers — after all, so many of them have been church members for ten, twenty, or more years. But soon we discover that beneath polite facades and sober faces there is a real uncertainty and confusion as to who Jesus Christ is. Besides, it troubles them that they should be so anxious and troubled when others seem to be so sure.

Our previous discussions have made it clear that the line does not necessarily run between believers and unbelievers, or the committed and the skeptical. The continuing problem of sin and unbelief is forever with us, and the believer is one who often struggles against his own unbelief. As we have indicated, the chief purpose of adults in attending study groups is not just to acquire knowledge or gain information, but to struggle with their faith under the guise of rationalism, moralism, and skepticism. It often happens that when the " believer " removes the mask of piety and thinks for himself he is faced with the skeptic's dilemma of meaninglessness and a terrible longing to believe. So, it is the task of Christian education, as we shall see later, to help adults to express their unbelief, bring it into the open, acknowledge it, wrestle with it, and learn to live in a continuous need of renewal at the hands of God.

Secondly, we want to make the point clear that Christian education by itself does not convert people. To claim this is to assume that a learner can be brought to an experience of conversion by another person, and further, that educators can or should anticipate the kind of person another human being should become. The point we want to emphasize is that in an educational situation it is highly probable that a person may be confronted, perhaps for the first time, with a penetrating message of the Christian faith, and respond to it in faith. This is not to push Christian education out of its proper function in relation to preaching or evangelism. It is true that teaching and preaching are functionally distinct. Traditionally, preaching is regarded as the proclamation of the kerygma and represents the grace of God, whereas teaching, or *didachē*, is referred to as the interpretation of the kerygma and represents the truth of God. But this does not mean that the two should be isolated from each other, or that one should be subordinated to the other. We create a false dichotomy by reasoning that preaching and teaching should go on independently, and by tenaciously holding to the view that one is superior to the other. Much of what was said about man and his faith is quite as relevant to Christian education as it is to preaching and social outreach. We often forget that educators write, teach, and lead to Christian influence as much as the preachers and evangelists do. Furthermore, in a total ministry to the total personality any sharp line between the various functions of the church's ministry is not only a superficial boundary, but unrecognizable, and even uncalled for.

INTERPRETING THE CHRISTIAN FAITH

Once adults have taken the initial step in joining the church or have entered into a relationship with God by confession of faith in Jesus Christ, their faith can grow and increase, and we believe that in an educational situation this is not only possible but highly probable. By growth we do not mean that there is an unbroken upward advance in spiritual life, but that each day the resources of faith are being restored and strengthened by God as man turns away from himself to God and receives his gift of acceptance and reconciliation. God in his giving of himself in love and forgiveness is constantly calling man into newness and growth.

" Do not be conformed to this world," Paul says, " but be transformed by the renewal of your mind, that you may prove what is the will of God, what is good and acceptable and perfect." (Rom. 12:2.) For Paul, " mind " means the " inmost self " or the true self. He writes, " Our inner nature is being renewed every day " (II Cor. 4:16) and points out that minds can be transformed by the renewal of the mind (repentance), through the power of the Spirit. This renewal, which is a new understanding, is given to the mind. It is not man's achievement but the gift of the Spirit.

An intellectual and active layman explained the meaning of " joining the church " and the necessity of Christian nurture as follows:

" Does one have a ' new life ' after being converted to Christianity or after confirming his infant baptism? I know the answer is yes, but the indefinable quantity then becomes — What is a ' new life '?

" Consider our lives for a moment. We are very much timeoriented, and our conscious self knows that one cannot stop the clock, or undo a thing done, or take back a spoken word. Thus a

vow or oath of any serious nature we consciously utter is a part
of us and will influence our lives. If you agree to this, then to have
full agreement between you and me we must only consider whether
an ' influenced life ' is a ' new life.'

" The military orders, perhaps rivaling religious orders in secular history, tradition, and background generally require that the
recruit swear his allegiance to defend with his all the tenents of
his order. Does he have a new life? Well, we know his daily life
probably does have a different schedule and round of activities. In
training, his skills to recognize the enemy as well as how to fight
him under direction or on a hand-to-hand basis are developed. On
active duty the recruit, now a soldier, will have many decisions to
make. Does not his oath or vow and his training influence each
decision? We agreed earlier that it would. In combat the soldier
has many life-or-death decisions to make that will influence both
himself and his enemy. He probably won't be conscious of it, but
his every previous movement will have conditioned him to cope
with the situation at hand and will influence to some extent his
decision.

" Would a person who did not take the soldier's oath respond
the same way? Maybe. But wouldn't he be a civilian and therefore
without the soldier's training, awareness, and obligation, and
therefore likely to have a completely different response? If the
action brought death or glory to our soldier or our civilian,
wouldn't the observer's response and rationalization of the affair
be different too? I think so and conclude that the soldier's life is
a ' new life ' initiated and influenced by his early taking of an
oath and its effects on his total experience thereafter. Could our
soldier predict what his ' new life ' would actually mean to him?
No. Man cannot foretell the future. He will only know when his
life after his oath, his ' new life ' period, is fulfilled and his experiences are behind him.

" This analogy may seem to degrade to secular terms the glorious
meaning of a ' new life ' after conversion to Christianity. But with
your understanding of Christian living, I hope it helps clarify the
theologians' meaning of a ' new life ' in Christ."

This analogy seems to be inadequate in conveying the real
meaning of becoming a member of the community of faith —

the church. However, we are offering it as an example of how laymen may think of themselves in need of a mature faith.

Thus repentance is not an act that takes place once for all, but it is a continuous " renewal of the mind " in the life of faith. It is a continual transformation made possible through faith in Jesus Christ. Therefore, it is the task of the church to provide the guidance that adults need in order to grow in such faith.

If Christian understanding comes with faith and is a gift of God's grace in Jesus Christ, can such knowledge be communicated through study or through the educational process? And further, if education employs reason for understanding certain truths, what place does rational thought have in communicating such faith?

Although communicating faith as an act of God's grace can hardly be referred to as " educational," it does not exempt us from the necessity of making an effort to interpret and explain the content of the knowledge that is given with the Christian faith as we understand it in the Scriptures, and bring it to the conscious knowledge of adults. We recall that the apostolic education of the early church under the Holy Spirit, according to Paul and others, was to explain the believers to themselves, to discipline them, to show them the nature of their faith, its impact upon their character, and its consequences in human destiny. The same is our task today. So, in order to help adults grow in Christian knowledge, they need to have an understanding of themselves and of the Christian faith in order that they may enter more fully into the heritage of knowledge and faith that belongs uniquely to the church.

Hence, it is proper to speak of the function of Christian education as interpreting the content of the Christian faith in such a way that those who hear it can increase their understanding. Interpretation implies communication, and we interpret in order to facilitate understanding. We are well aware that this task is not free from the difficulties that beset the communication of knowledge described above, and we have only to read Paul's letters to understand how difficult the task was. Therefore, the communication of the Christian faith calls for a distinctive kind of education.

It has been suggested that there are two types of understanding, namely, a " knowledge about " as well as " knowledge of " (or, in Bultmann's terms, an *existential* as well as an *existentiell* knowledge). Although the two should not be separated, for the sake of clarity we shall discuss them under different headings and point out their unique role in adult Christian education. First, in order to guide adults to an understanding of God's grace in Jesus Christ, Christian education must take the responsibility of transmitting or imparting a body of objective knowledge that is necessary to understanding and entering into the Christian faith.

As we have already indicated in the previous chapters, in most instances adults are ignorant of the simple facts about the Bible, the church, and the basic Christian beliefs. Once in a study group when the question was raised as to what eventually happened to Moses, the answer was, " According to the movie [*The Ten Commandments*], he died on the mountain and God buried him there." Whether the answer is correct or not is beside the point. The significant fact is that these days adults can know Biblical " facts " without reading the Bible. An untold number of people have no knowledge of the simple chronological order of events in the Bible. Many have hazy ideas about the events of the life, death, and resurrection of Christ. Very few are able to tell the life story of Jesus as it is recorded in the Synoptic Gospels.

We meet people who use language that they do not understand. They recite creedal definitions and prayers without comprehension of their content. Here is a layman who has been the chairman of numerous church committees and has spent endless hours planning each big fund-raising event, who is actually repelled by the sacrament of the Holy Communion because he considers it a pagan and meaningless ritual. For many people who have poured endless hours of time and energy in planning for the annual church bazaars or fairs, a true Christian life remains a dark mystery. Adults need to have an objective understanding of the faith the church proclaims. They should be led to a factual knowledge of the Bible story, the history of the church, its sacraments, its creeds, and its liturgy. They need to learn how to participate with understanding in acts of worship. They need to have a working knowledge of the church as the body of Christ and its mission in the world as a suffering servant.

It is fair to say that unless adults mature in their knowledge and understanding of the Christian faith, we may expect them to be open to the wiles of error, and to distorted and dangerous ideas about God and his relation to man. The church cannot afford to leave its adults comfortable in their ignorance and egocentricity, disposing their loyalty whereever and whenever they please. Neither can it be satisfied with having adults whose thinking is tainted with queer and distorted ideas borrowed from astrology, spiritualism, reincarnation, Bahaism, or Zen Buddhism.

After having said this, we now have to face the question whether acquisition of knowledge will actually make an adult Biblically faithful and more Christian, or at least more sympathetic to the Christian faith. We all meet people who do know a great deal about Christianity and still reject it.

Indeed, imparting information is not communicating the Christian faith, but it may be true that we cannot communicate our faith without imparting certain information and facts that form the foundation of the Christian faith. It is true that we should not be satisfied with imparting information for the sake of satisfying the curiosity of people or answering intellectual questions. In Christian education of adults, we cannot be satisfied with transmitting information for information's sake, since God's disclosure of himself in Jesus Christ is not synonymous with subject matter. Our ultimate aim is that people be believers and grow in their faith. Commitment is more than intellectual assent, it is response to God, the Father of Jesus Christ. It involves a passionate risking, an involvement in the affairs of humanity. People need to engage in both, for the church needs believing as well as informed and thinking adults. But the important fact is that belief in historical facts is not to be confused with the Christian faith. People should know the distinction, and realize that, as Pascal put it, " The knowledge of God is very far from the love of God." It is true that the least we can say is that some acquaintance with the Christian tradition is essential if one is to know about the object of his search, but we also believe that it is highly probable that imparting or transmitting of such knowledge may open the way for an encounter with God, perhaps even for the first time, and lead adults to participate in the events in which God revealed his nature and purpose.

Secondly, Christian education of adults should be concerned with a knowledge of the Christian faith, or an existential interpretation of the Christian faith, or as Brunner puts it, " spiritual understanding " of the faith.

As we have already indicated, this kind of knowledge is not a set of propositions or a body of academic information and facts to be transmitted or learned. Rather, it is a special kind of knowledge — a saving knowledge, as it is called — that comes through faith in Jesus Christ. The nature of this saving faith, we have explained, is the unreserved commitment of the whole person — his mind, heart, and will to God's grace in Jesus Christ. It is the acceptance of God's grace that is also the acceptance of one's own sin at the same time. We have repeatedly stated that the way of faith that is the basis of spiritual understanding is made possible to man by God's act of grace, that it is a gift of the Holy Spirit, and that the how of it remains a mystery.

After we have said all this, the question is still with us, namely, How is this faith to be interpreted and communicated?

It is very important for Christian educators to know how laymen understand themselves. The previous chapters gave us a glimpse of how modern average Protestants understand themselves in their quest for meaning and in their faith and uncertainties. Therefore, Christian education should be concerned not merely with answering questions at the intellectual level but with interpreting man to himself in his quest for meaning, in his anxiety, guilt, doubt, in his concern with the world, in his striving for power, in his reliance on human reason, in his confidence in material things, in his quest for the " good life."

To be more specific, adults should come to an understanding that their experiences of life are not merely psychological, cultural, or biological, but spiritual. Certain types of experiences, such as sudden illness, death, suffering, or awareness of guilt, doubt, and meaninglessness, make people conscious of their tensions and anxiety and force them to ask questions of serious concern. Further, they are aware of the ambiguity of human loyalties and the fruitlessness of human effort, which seeks fulfillment through man's powers alone. It is therefore the duty of Christian education to interpret these experiences theologically and help adults to understand themselves in their relation to God, to self, and to their fellowman. Here a word of caution is necessary. Christian education is not to deal with deep-rooted guilt-anxiety problems, for these belong to the domain of the psychiatrist. It can only recognize them and refer them to those who are qualified to deal with them professionally.

What we are saying is that Christian education should be able to describe the nature of man and thus enable him to know himself as he truly is: a child of God, created in his image, yet alienated from God by his pride and selfishness, and living against his destiny. Further, it interprets the consequences of his egocentricity, rebellion, and idolatry in personal, social, economic, and political spheres. Nonetheless, Christian education must be able to help man to know himself as he is meant to be: that he is not forsaken to self-destruction but called back to communion with God through the life, death, and the resurrection of Jesus Christ. This involves not merely bringing man's existence to the gospel message, but bringing the Christian revelation to man as it is witnessed to in the Bible and the church. It is actually an invitation to participate in the new being in Christ.

Moreover, Christian education should be able to explain the quality of life that springs from ultimate commitment to God in Jesus Christ. Adults need to increase their working knowledge of the basic concepts of the Christian faith: God, man, sin, guilt, Christ, life, death, eternal life. As we have seen, it is a sobering but instructive experience to hear adults express their concepts of the Christian faith and practice. There is a denunciation of sin and an approval of virtue, but it is often a pious or moralistic substitute for a real knowledge of human predicament; there is a fervent search for knowledge and the acquiring of information, but often without reliance upon the redeeming grace of God; there is a firm resolution in sharing a good cause, but it is often unrelated to a real discipleship in a common life of faith and grace. Most nominal Christians do not have the slightest idea of the real relationship between being a Christian and one's attitude toward work, one's understanding of love, one's involvement in human affairs, including politics and social concern.

Christian education must show what the life of ultimate devotion means in a wide range of human concern, for as we have already seen, we cannot assume that Christians automatically know the demands of God's purpose and will. Adults should be helped to understand the relevance of the Christian faith to the great issues of our time, from nationalism to racial conflict, from cold war to social injustices, from population explosion to public morality. They should be able to distinguish between ways of God and ways of man, and consider what faithfulness to God demands in social, political, and economic affairs. They should explore the deeper implications of the Christian faith in homes, offices, schools, clubs, factories, and wherever the Christian people live and work. A word of caution is necessary here. When we speak of the relevance of the Christian faith to the issues of life, we do not mean merely adding or applying it to the issues of everyday life from one situation to another like a packaged truth. The idea of application is sterile, if not deadly, when it is understood in a mechanical way. It has meaning only when the gospel message faces man with God's redeeming love in such a way that it enables him to venture forth into life and risk the precariousness of transferring conviction into action, in order to learn what it is to suffer, to risk death, and to know what it is to live again.

Now we have come to the point of meeting our second challenge, namely, if Christian knowledge is given in the experience of faith, what place does reason have in such interpretation?

Here it is important for us to keep in mind that there is a distinction between reason that is implied in the experience of faith and reason, which is a matter of speculation and is separated from faith. The foregoing discussions have shown that adults struggle with both. In the following pages, we shall attempt to discuss the importance of reason in interpreting the Christian faith.

First, it is necessary to realize that the nature of faith is such that it impels the believer to seek understanding with his mind. In other words, reason can never be absent from faith. The questions adults ask are an indication that they need help in developing a reasonable faith. Thus, the questions they ask so boldly and stubbornly are of utmost importance and we have to take them seriously lest our discussions end with all sorts of religious and nonreligious nonsense. Christian education should guide and encourage adults to expand their thinking without enervating the mystery of faith; it should cultivate passion for truth without the atrophy of the wisdom and the power of the gospel; and it should develop, as Fry says, " bigness inside " without corrupting the judgment, both of faith and of reason. It is very easy to stifle the thinking of adults by driving them into a phobia of human wisdom and thus giving them an easy refuge in mystery in the face of intellectual inconvenience. As Fry says, Christian education should seek " to help the thinking man to think," and this can happen if we prevent obscurantism and help the laymen to strengthen their intellectual sinews. It is well to remember that conversion is not a matter of the will only, it is also a cognitive, intellectual process.

Secondly, we realize that intellectual inquiry may not lead directly to faith, but we also know that faith does not happen without the struggle of reason. As a matter of fact, apart from rigorous inquiry, anyone can believe anything. The great questions that men can ask with their minds are questions that may be raised by both philosophy and theology as some great theologians of our day, such as Tillich and Bultmann, have tried to show. It is true we cannot and should not indulge in questions of metaphysical meanings that can easily obscure the basic issues of the Christian faith, nor is it wise to be involved in meeting every specific charge. To do so is to engage in secondary matters that are not pertinent to our purpose. On the other hand, we cannot remain aloof from contemporary intellectual struggle either. To do so is to make the Christian message hopelessly remote from those inside as well as outside the community of faith.

To argue that faith does not ignore any scientific knowledge in order to be a believer or to prove that faith preserves and maintains the true interest of reason is not, we admit, the primary task of Christian education; but it is a necessary task. Here let us make our point clear. We are not pleading for " intellectualized Christianity," nor are we accommodating the truth of the Christian faith to the truth of reason. As a matter of fact, we dare not weaken the " foolishness " and the " offense " of the gospel. The point we want to emphasize is that we often spend time helping people to get rid of rigid dogmatism, narrow legalism, superstitions and distorted ideas that have become substitutes for a Christian life. Granted that all this is necessary and urgent, in our time there is a special need for intellectual honesty in order to be able to face the challenge that comes to the church through various fields of the modern culture. Laymen should go through the agony of theological reflections as well as disciplined Christian thought. They should be helped to think as honestly and as carefully as they can. This is not easy, for thinking and believing require hard work and rigorous discipline of heart and mind.

Further, in order to be able to interpret our faith and make it comprehensible to the inquiring minds, Christian educators have to undergo the discipline of mastering its intellectual structures and its problems. Christian faith is intellectually exciting, and we must endeavor to present its intellectual challenge to those who are ready to respond to it in intellectual conversation that commends itself as true. Meanwhile, we shall rest assured that as long as faith refuses to absolutize reason because it is set within the life of the finite man and accepts the inevitability of reason's use as a gift from God, the tension between the two can remain desirable and necessary for the life of faith.

Thirdly, intellectual struggle may enlarge the field of mystery and hence widen and deepen the range of quest. Further, objective knowledge — facts and information — can enrich the context in which questions may be raised and new insights gained. Christian education should enable adults to acquire a wisdom that learns the limits of human knowledge and recognizes that at the end man must face what it means to live in a world where the answers to life's questions — of life, death, evil, suffering — are not obvious and where he does not control the life and destiny of mankind.

The modern adult may live in the light of increasing knowledge, but he must be helped to face a question of the life he is going to lead. This is a matter of personal commitment in a world where the dimensions of life are deeper and higher than their surface appearance, " which has been frozen by rationalism into an icy solidity, giving those who seek a firm footing upon it a false sense of security. The ice is not very thick; the ocean beneath it is deep and tempestuous; and the sun above is warm and melting." [21]

Thus it is hoped that the restless urge for personal meaning may drive our intellectuals out of the comfort of academic knowledge to an awareness of the mystery of life, which is something more than an unknown region not yet explored by an advancing technology. We hope that as adults get involved in intellectual struggle, they may discover the inadequacies of their reasoning and thus be driven out of despair to questions that pertain to the ultimate meaning of life: " What shall I do to have faith? " " What is the basic meaning of life? " " Is life worth living? " " Why did God create me? " No one can really avoid seeking answers to the basic issues of life, and the core of Christian faith is God's answer to these questions. We must continually keep pushing the mind to the questions that Christian faith is attempting to answer about the meaning of existence, the mystery of man's ultimate significance, the meaning of death, grace, forgiveness, reconciliation.

Thus our answer to the challenge of the importance of reason in interpreting the Christian faith is in agreement with Fry, who says: " God has graced the intellectual areas of spiritual (hidden) life. Here is one place where God has dealings with man as surely as he does in market, office, gas station, or before the television set. Such a belief grows out of the simple evangelical conviction of God's saving work. It happens in the mind and its conceptual activities if anywhere at all." [22] And we realize that whatever we teach or learn is not by the power of our minds but " a disclosure by God's gracious condescension." [23] Therefore, we hope that God who has granted to man the gift of knowledge will also, through the Holy Spirit, supply continuous meaning and enlightenment.

A BIG QUESTION

So we come to the big question that is put to us in the following statement:

A friend of the author expressed the following challenge after having led an extensive program of Christian education for adults in his church. " All we have is a group of well-informed, educated, unconverted laymen who criticize the sermons, ask for changes in the celebration of the sacraments, demand explanations for the choice of hymns, challenge the decisions of official boards, and downgrade the church organization. Where do we go from here? "

What is implied in this statement is the big question, Are we justified in saying that Christian education can lead adults to repentance? Or, can Christian education touch the deep, corelike resistance of adults by the message of the gospel?

In meeting this challenge, we shall make the following observations:

People do witness to the transforming aspect of their religious faith and action. For instance, let us examine some of their comments. " I was inspired, if nothing else! " The word " inspired " may mean many things in the vocabulary of laymen. It may mean to be encouraged, to be supported, or to be lifted in morale. But inspiration is also interpreted as an experience of being grasped by a new understanding or a new meaning. " I was suddenly made aware of what was already there and I did not know it. It is like the force of gravity that was there, but people did not know it until they were made aware of it."

Laymen often speak of having gained new insight. " This session was a breakthrough," one layman reports convincingly. " I never knew it until it dawned on me suddenly."

Should we not understand insight as that experience in which facts fall into new meaning through a flash of understanding? May we not believe that this is a time when eternal truth is disclosed and apprehended? Time and again people have reported that when new ideas and insights penetrated life, their old ideas and traditions were shattered, and suddenly they were faced with an experience of some new truth with new meanings. " I'm really changed." " I've a new way of looking at myself and my neighbor." " I'm not afraid to be friendly with people." " I feel free and without fear, and I don't care what others think of me." " I feel free to think and to ask questions." " I feel free to enjoy life."

When adults report that they have seen something new and different that has changed their outlook on life; when they say that in some way they have come to terms with themselves and feel their conflicts resolved, then we can say that they have learned — or that learning has taken place. This kind of learning is not a purely rational process; it is a special kind of learning — a special kind of wisdom imparted by the Holy Spirit. This is not to say that reason has no place, as Brunner says:

> The thinking subject is not eliminated by faith, it is not overwhelmed and pushed aside, but it is claimed by God. The self is not denuded of dignity, but it is forced to vacate its position of sovereignty, which it had usurped, and dishonestly appropriated, and it is set in its proper place.[24]

This kind of change is only a beginning or a sign of deeper changes in the hidden depths of the human spirit. As Brunner puts it, even though faith does not spring from thought, it begins " with rethinking and with a change of outlook." [25]

Educationally, we are not in a position to explain or describe the subtle and profound changes of the inner life.

Even the person himself cannot trace this new learning in logical steps or attribute it to some academic knowledge that has been learned. He knows it has come from beyond his thought and will — and " despite himself." Further, he is aware of the fact that it is a gift and that because it is God's gift, it results in a new perspective and a new way of life. What has actually happened is that God has acted upon the heart and mind of the person.

It is usually believed that Christian education is evaluated in terms of what happens to adults because of their new learning or new insights. In this light, we state once more that the test of the Christian education of adults is whether or not it leads toward the inexplicable change of mind called repentance. The foregoing discussion has made us aware of the fact that adults do experience change of mind, and that they " grow in knowledge and grace." Further, we do believe that " the fruit of the Spirit is love, joy, peace, patience, kindness, goodness, faithfulness, gentleness, self-control " (Gal. 5:22-23), and that these are the gifts of God's grace; but we also realize that what happens to man when he is grasped by the power of the Holy Spirit no one knows. No one can really describe or evaluate the new life, for it is a complete reorientation of the entire personality. Thus, we agree with Rachel Henderlite, who believes that we can recognize the fruits of the Spirit, but to attempt to measure them in the life of an individual is to reject the doctrine of grace. We cannot evaluate the new life, but can point out God's longing for communion with men.[26]

After we have said all this, the most important point we want to make is that God works through men in ways that go beyond anything we can think of or confine within our educational or theological systems. All we can do is to hope that God, through the Holy Spirit, may reach the hearts and minds of those who attend study groups with expectation.

WITNESSING THE CHRISTIAN FAITH

The Christian faith is of such nature that it demands witnessing. Those who share in the church's ministry stand in need of growth in faith as well as of meaningful response to the world's need for salvation. Laymen should realize that " they are the church " in the Biblical sense, the people of God out in the world to play a vital part in the mission of the church. Thus the church must be concerned with the maturity of its adults if they are to be effective witnesses. We are justified, therefore, in saying that the ultimate purpose of Christian adult education is to prepare the people of God to share with the world God's redeeming and reconciling love in Jesus Christ in order that they may share in the task of evangelism which is ever the role of the church. " But you are a chosen race, a royal priesthood, a holy nation, God's own people, that you may declare the wonderful deeds of him who called you out of darkness into his marvelous light. Once you were no people but now you are God's people; once you had not received mercy but now you have received mercy." (I Peter 2:9-10.) The doctrine of " the priesthood of all believers " means that the community of faith has a particular responsibility to think through the meaning of its message so that it can share the truth on which its life depends and make known to the world where it stands and why.

In the familiar words of Brunner, the Christian message is both gift and task; it cannot be possessed unless it is shared. " I don't know how to witness my faith because I don't know very much about it," says the layman. " Besides, I have no occasion to speak about it. I don't think people are interested in listening, anyway! " To bear witness is more than just speaking to people about our faith. It is to live in conformity with it. Increasingly, we realize that Christian witness demands the actual involvement with the secular world that Hans-Ruedi Weber, of the World Council of

Churches, refers to as "worldly holiness." It occurs on the level of nonverbal communication through the lives and actions of Christians as God directs and sustains them.

After a concentrated study on the nature and the mission of the church, the reaction of one group was, "Where were we all those years?" Sometimes the danger of some study groups is that in discussing and reading about the Christian faith, adults think that they are being Christian. Many laymen talk about religious issues in politics but shy at commitment to any particular struggle. They expound the major issues of social injustices without taking any steps that will lead to a decisive act. They have strong feelings of sympathy toward suffering, hunger, and poverty, and even feel that they have suffered, but without any desire to participate in any action. As someone has said, "Many of our laymen are like the spectator at a football game who has all the anxiety, all the despair, all the joy of victory, but none of the bruises and fatigues of the combat." Thus, the church should help adults to be discriminative about what action is worthwhile, and it should introduce them to the kinds of redemptive experiences through which new insights are gained and new truths are discovered. Thus, it is the responsibility of the church, and therefore the function of Christian education, to help its members not only to think through the meaning of their faith in order to give a clear account of the Christian message in words, but actually to involve them actively in social action. They should be encouraged to undertake a courageous and responsible involvement in political, economic, and social matters.

Naturally, this will involve risks. There is the risk of being misunderstood both outside and inside the church as adults refuse to ignore the "secular" world and even appreciate its prophetic challenge. There is the risk of being called "the ugly American." And there is the risk of having to act and speak with explorative tentativeness and honesty instead of with self-possessed assurance and comfortable complacency. Thus, the new life in Christ to which we are invited calls us to be evangelists — all of us. But this is not a popular image. It is the image of a servant, and those who share in the church's ministry must be willing to speak and act as a servant people of the Servant Lord.

Let us now return to another aspect of Christian witnessing. The community of faith — the church — has a particular responsibility, namely, to be concerned with the maturity of its members for effective teaching in the church. Robert McAfee Brown points out that every Christian is to be a " learned minister " and that the Protestant conception of the " learned ministry " should be placed alongside " the priesthood of all believers." [27] Those who are called to the responsibility of sharing the church's ministry stand in need not only of passionate intellectual search but of sharing and interpreting the faith effectively and with conviction to others within the community. In the church there is a clear duty for novices in the mystery of our faith who can take the initiative and bring still others within the fold.

Our discussion has brought us to still another important phase of the life of faith. Christian faith is not a life of isolation. It is set in the community of faith, the church, in which man finds his fulfillment in the fellowship of discipleship and worship. William Temple said, " Philosophy seeks knowledge for the sake of understanding, while religion seeks knowledge for the sake of worship." [28]

Christian education is not an end in itself. It does not claim to make any man a Christian; it is a hope that in an educational situation, adults will grow in an understanding of their destiny as heirs of God's grace and thus come to a decision of repentance. Therefore such expectation should be nourished by roots that go deeper than study, namely, worship and witness. It is the responsibility of Christian education to help adults realize the importance of the experience of corporate worship, to give them a clear understanding of the Word and the sacraments as means of grace, and to help them participate in the common life of the Christian fellowship. Learning takes place in the context of the church as a supporting and sustaining fellowship for those who confront the world and come back for further study and renewal.

The educated and well-informed laymen who prefer study groups to the service of worship and so keep away from worship should cause us great alarm. On the other hand, those who alarm us because of their criticism of sermons, sacraments, and hymns have already begun to think " charismatically."

◇ IV ◇

SUGGESTIONS FOR CHRISTIAN ADULT
EDUCATION IN THE CHURCH

Although this chapter is not intended to present a structural plan for organizing and conducting adult classes in the church, it seems appropriate that a few suggestions be made to implement some of the concerns expressed in earlier chapters. We have to keep in mind that both organization and methods should arise out of a particular situation and must serve only as means to an end. But before we discuss the issue, we shall turn to the problem of motivation.

MOTIVATION AND LEARNING

One of the most important factors in learning is motivation. Generally speaking, adults have little motivation to learn, especially when they are not facing a crisis or are not prompted and stimulated to want to learn and explore. Thus, the problem of motivation remains a difficult one in adult education.

How can we motivate the adults to want to learn? How can we help them to realize the importance of study and thus encourage them to participate in study groups? These are not easy questions to answer, because so many adults believe that they know more than children and that they have passed the phase of life that offers natural enthusiasm for new ideas and the native sense of wonderment over the mystery of life. Furthermore, most adults believe that attending Sunday morning service is sufficient for their spiritual growth, and so there is little motivation for them to want to be involved in study groups.

In this discussion, our problem is not with those adults who do not attend study classes. Rather, we are concerned with those who are already in study groups, and our problem is how to motivate them and hence improve the teaching-learning situation. There are at least two considerations that have a crucial bearing on motivating the adults to seek knowledge and to want to learn.

First, all thinking about education must take into account the needs of adults. The question is how can we determine this. There are universal needs of humanity that should be taken seriously. For instance, Thomas' Four Wishes (security, response, recognition, new experience), set in an old classic discussion, are still considered helpful in an understanding of the basic needs of human beings. Further, we realize that adults have needs and that they are related to age-group interests and concerns. However, these needs and interests are so complex and so numerous that if, without discrimination, we make them the basis for learning or understanding the Christian faith, we are allowing them to determine and hence limit the possibility of what can and should be learned. It is true that all thinking about Christian adult education must seriously consider where adults are in their needs and interests, but it is also important to recognize the context out of which they arise. Needs and interests of adults are to a large extent conditioned by economic, political, and social forces of the society and are instilled in the individual through the influence of home, school, and community, and affect his attitudes and motivations. This by no means ignores the social situations in which adults live, for the truth of Christian revelation is known only in relation to real life; and to have a real concern for the people in their moods, the overtones and undertones of their existence, is the central concern of the church itself. What we have to keep in mind is that these needs and interests are not ends in themselves but are means toward understanding adults, and hence are of service to our knowledge of the Christian doctrine of man.

Another way of looking at needs is in terms of the human situation or man's predicament. Sufficient evidence has been presented in previous chapters to indicate the needs out of which adults raise their questions and express their doubts. These are universal concerns which everyone is experiencing just by virtue of being human. They are shared by everyone and pertain to everyone, and yet they do not belong to everyone in the same sense. Each adult faces his own particular situation and makes his own decisions. This means that we cannot just talk about some generalized concept of needs or be satisfied with the universality of man's situation. It is the concrete individual, living here and now, who is the crux of the Christian message and the focus of faith.

Another factor in effective learning is a sense of success and achievement. Adults are motivated to learn when they know they have learned and when they feel that their knowledge has been expanded, that they have achieved the goal they had in mind, and that something unusual has happened to them. It gives them satisfaction when they realize that facts and information can be learned and Christian doctrine can be understood intellectually. We know laymen who develop keen intellectual capacity and who would pass a rigorous test in Biblical knowledge or theology without any difficulty. In short, adults gain a sense of accomplishment when they feel they have made the knowledge their very own. This kind of achievement motivates them to have confidence in themselves as capable of understanding and responding to ideas and situations.

Educationally, this is what we call learning, and we have referred to it as perceiving meaning, gaining insight, which may also be a sign of deeper changes in the self — the change of motives and attitudes. This inner change, as was stated before, is not something that has been " learned " ; it is a gift — a gift because it is not man's achievement, and man himself has not worked for it. So, when the adults think in terms of learning as an accomplishment, it is well for them to keep in mind the difference between the intellectual understanding of the Christian faith that any person can learn and the understanding through faith that is the gift of the Holy Spirit.

In summary, in order to motivate adults to want to learn, we must keep the following in mind. First, what they need for study is not something that is merely interesting, amusing, or even desirable, but something that has meaning in the human situation. Secondly, such a study should be challenging enough to stimulate learning. Adults need to be challenged intellectually and spiritually in order to develop the passion for truth needed for spiritual maturity.

Types of Study

What should adults study? Let us agree, for the sake of the discussion, that no subject should be declared out of bounds. Sufficient evidence has been presented in the earlier chapters to indicate that since adults have numerous questions and diverse interests and needs, therefore a program of varied subjects is not only necessary but imperative. But before we discuss the subject matter more specifically, we would like to make the following observations. First, an indiscriminate emphasis on varied subjects soon finds us competing with general education. Bergevin, the architect of the Indiana Plan, points out that one of the pitfalls of Christian adult education is the use of slightly modified secular subject matter to the point that it " might often be any secular subject with a slightly recognizable religious twist to it." He goes on to say: " Learning flower arrangement and pottery-making may have a place in the cultural and educational pattern of our society. It is not, however, the job of the religious adult educator. When he tries to compete with such secular programs in order to interest people in the church by indirect methods, he is watering down the church's mission and educational purpose." [29] Thus, to reduce the content of the Christian faith to entertaining subjects or even psychological, philosophical, or sociological " material " is to weaken the Christian message; and, as Barth has charged, it is to treat the unfaith of the pagan seriously.

Secondly, choosing easy courses with simple answers is not only avoiding complex issues of life but also perpetuating the danger of easy belief in what is comforting and confining. For instance, a course based on a book like *Step by Step in Theology* (Association Press) may sound simple in that it may lead the student to the right answer, but such a modernized catechetical method can kill the imagination and perhaps never lead the student to a genuine struggle of mind and soul in his confrontation with the God of the Bible. Thus, simplicity is a nebulous and undefined quality, and we can make of it almost anything we will. The commonest error is the assumption that to be simple is to present easy and reassuring ideas and not disturb the hearers by the claims of the gospel and the basic problems of human existence. This is a kind of irresponsible simplicity that requires no thinking, no suffering, and no anxiety. It does not stimulate and fascinate and thus fortify the growth of the learning process. There are those who equate simplicity with the thought of a child and thus reduce the most profound truth to almost nonsense. Alfred North Whitehead once said, " Simple solutions are bogus solutions." Here we do not wish to imply that educators should use advanced academic or technical books and subject matter, thinking that this way they can stimulate the laymen. Indeed, highly academic subjects create barriers and deprive most adults of the meaning of the gospel message. It is true that many adults are still babes in Christ and need to be nourished on milk, but to keep them in a stage of " childhood innocence " is to deprive them of genuine growth in understanding of the Christian faith.

We are concerned to insist that the great doctrines of the Christian faith are not to be evaluated by the criterion of simplicity as long as simplicity remains an ambiguous concept and demands disavowal of thought. This should be resisted at all costs. However, if simplicity means intelligibility of thought, then the question is, How articulate is this simplicity? Those who teach are well aware of the fact that it requires a great deal of knowledge and a deep insight of the subject matter to be " simple." Furthermore, the more profound the subject, the less likelihood there is that it can be adequately formulated in simple terms. This is not to deny the simple folk and the less intellectual their knowledge. As a matter of fact, such knowledge may often come closer to God than a philosophical discussion or a sophisticated theological table talk. We should be concerned to awaken these people to the profundity of their own simplifications and allow for the differences of individual background, conceptual ability, and religious and educational experience.

Thus, in order to grow and learn, one has to struggle against odds and oppositions, to take risks, to experience uncertainties. After all, is not faith perpetual insecurity before God who claims our obedience?

Granting these warnings, what are the possibilities of " meeting the needs " of adults? How can we see our way through in a world that is rapidly changing, that is charged with unprecedented destructiveness of war, and that offers no relief from inexorable conflict of faith and reason, the instability of ethical standards, and the ever-changing forms of conformity? In this world and no other, the church is called to interpret its message, to help its adults to understand themselves and the world they live in, and to minister to the human society.

Enough examples have been given in the foregoing chapters to suggest what adults need to study. The courses may fall under general areas of the Bible, theology, church history, and social sciences; or another classification would be: religion and culture, nature of man, history and faith, and faith and reason. Regardless of how we classify the courses, the earlier chapters have confirmed that two important areas must be kept in mind: the Christian revelation and the human situation. This does not mean that we follow Tillich's " method of correlation," which develops the message-situation, or question-answer scheme, and claims that the Christian gospel provides " answers " to the problem of human existence. Granting that some correlative effort is always required, the nature of the Christian faith is such that it confronts people with questions of risk and doubt rather than furnishes them with answers to the perplexities of life. Thus Tillich's " method of correlation " is helpful when it warns us against giving answers to questions that are never actually asked. What we mean is that there are two starting points for any type of study. We may start with God's revelation in Jesus Christ as witnessed in the Bible and the church. The purpose of such an approach is that the adults may be confronted with this event and understand its meaning for their existence. Or we may begin with the crucial situations of life — with man, his problems, anxieties, doubts, faith, and unfaith. It is believed that since these are universal concerns, they are relevant for the Christian faith and should be seen in the light of the gospel. Let us be forthright by saying that, whatever the starting point, our ultimate purpose is to help adults to move beyond the world of self and away from mere talk about the Christian faith to a confrontation with the God of our Lord Jesus Christ.

Modern Arts

The study of the creative dimensions of culture — art, music, drama, fiction, poetry, theater — has been quite popular in recent years. The purpose of such study has been to find an entry into the contemporary mind in order to be able to present the Christain faith in terms intelligible to our age. Further, here again we find Tillich's " method of correlation " illuminating. Tillich, as we recall, looks to the arts and the philosophy of our time to discover the questions that our world is asking about many aspects of man's ultimate concern. For instance, poets, artists, and writers such as Arthur Miller, T. S. Eliot, Tennessee Williams, Albert Camus, Jean-Paul Sartre, Jean Anouilh, Picasso, and others, express the search for a meaning beyond rationality. They reveal the soul-shaking chaos that religious piety, reason, and science so artificially mask. Artists give the modern man an image of himself that he would prefer to bypass rather than face. In summary, it is believed that modern arts can speak more powerfully than does the " contemporary gospel." They can speak with disarming frankness and explain man to himself in his situation of guilt and anxiety. Therefore, the purpose is to help laymen to discover the questions that the world is asking about man's estrangement from himself and from his fellowman, about his flight from life, his search for meaning.

Many laymen ignore modern arts and link them with sensuality, worldliness, and distortion of truth; some read and study avidly without understanding the actual meaning involved; a few have a good grasp of what the artists are trying to convey; and still others are indifferent, wondering what all this has to do with the Christian faith.

The author believes that adults need to be personally acquainted with some of the areas of culture in which questions of various aspects of man's ultimate concern are emerging, but in order to get a theological grasp of artistic, psychological, and philosophical materials, we need to keep the following in mind.

First, we should be able to understand the issues that are raised by these artists and writers and reflect upon the answers they give in the light of the Christian faith.

Secondly, we should guard against adjusting the Christian message in such a way as to fit its answer to questions that are not actually asked. A friend of the author's was told by the writer of a well-known novel that he was surprised, if not alarmed, at the way " religious people " misinterpret what he is really trying to convey.

Thirdly, people find some kind of temporary moral catharsis in reading modern literature and studying modern art. For instance, here is a layman who sees himself as Willy Loman in his effort to find out who he really is. What happens is that the layman finds a temporary relief, but actually his real problems are untouched.

Science and Religion

The conflict between science and religion and its moral implications still remains a very real and prominent problem to a large majority of adults. The church cannot afford to sweep aside science as the scientists can sweep aside religion. Whether we like it or not, scientific knowledge and technological skills provide the backbone of the world in which adults have to live and act. Further, it becomes more and more evident that with the increasing control by natural science of the physical world and the profound influence upon the processes of mind by social sciences such as anthropology, sociology, psychology, and so on, man is gaining new powers to create what is good for himself, and he assumes responsibility for the direction of his life and destiny. As a result God makes less and less difference to the human situation, and man becomes more and more the " master of his fate " and the " captain of his soul."

First, laymen should have an understanding of the fact that as scientists, technicians, industrialists, research workers, engineers, teachers, etc., they are set in the world not only as co-workers with God in the continuing work of his creation, but are involved in an enterprise that seeks to transform man's earthly existence and hence shape the destiny of mankind. It is therefore important to help adults to examine the ultimate purpose on which the enterprise is based and the convictions by which it is operated and supported. They should understand their work as an important vocation — a way in which men respond to the call of God in and through daily work. Since all truth is God's truth, even the scientist's work is an important part of man's service to God and can offer positive and significant service to humanity.

Thus, in our program of adult education we should make room for courses based on the meaning of vocation and man's attitude toward it. There may also be professional or occupational groups who would meet to discuss their common problems in the light of the Christian faith. Such experiments are being made in a few churches, and it is possible that the pattern may be followed on a larger scale.

Secondly, adults should be helped to understand that there is no inherent conflict between science and religion. They are different ways of man's understanding and responding to reality; therefore any quarrel between them should be unnecessary. Conflict occurs when they interfere with each other's domain, or when one or the other claims to have exclusive truth as the only possible truth of the world.

Scientific discussion cannot be said to contradict our theological and Biblical thought except when we are rash enough to make pseudopsychological assertions about events in the world of nature. To defend the pale relics of antiquity against a twentieth-century view of the world and of God's relation to it is to drive adults away from the church. It is true that the church must hold fast to the content of its faith; yet it is also true that it lives in immediate and present response to its Lord. We should be able to face the question of what nature is and how God is the creator, judge, and redeemer of the creative life. Tension between scientific reason and faith will remain with us, but the basic disposition should be toward resolving the tension as adults think together about the meaning and implications of the doctrine of creation and man's place in the world as a responsible human being.

Religious Relativism

If our ultimate aim in Christian education is to prepare or train adults to witness their faith to those outside the faith, the problem of religious relativism becomes inevitable.

We have stated before that many adults believe Christianity is a religion among others, or that " Christianity is a good religion." There are also those who find the exclusiveness of Christianity or the " scandal of particularity " a stumbling block. " After all," they claim, " God is known in a thousand different ways, and ' he did not leave himself without witness ' " (Acts 14:17).

To try to prove or validate the gospel message on rational or empirical grounds is not only unwise but impossible. Besides, it is impossible and even dangerous to try to convince someone by words or instruction, for even a careful discussion or argument does not ordinarily bring men into divine encounter with God. In the final analysis, adults must come to their own faith in Jesus Christ through the witness of the Holy Spirit and the testimony of Bible and church.

This leads us to suggest the following areas for study.

Adults should have a thorough understanding of the reasons for Christianity's being in the world. It is none other than to give meaning to human history. But since Christianity without the church is unthinkable, it is important to understand the nature and mission of the church as the body of Christ in the sense that it carries on the work of Christian history until the coming of the new age. This means that the Bible and the church are dependent on each other and cannot be separated. The church determined the canon of the Bible, while the canon serves as the source of preaching, teaching, creeds, confessions, and even personal religious experience.

Such an understanding includes a study of the story the Bible tells: the story of the " mighty acts " of God in history in and through his people, culminating in the life, death, and resurrection of Jesus Christ. It includes a study of the creeds, confessions, and liturgies of the church, and of the truths to which they point. It means a thorough understanding of the message of God's reconciling love in Jesus Christ that should be carried on among men and a genuine comprehension of what it means to become servants and thus fulfill our mission in life. Thus it is hoped that those who are confronted with this testimony will understand the meaning of their existence in terms of this great event.

Adults must wrestle with the problem of the universality of religion and the uniqueness of the Christian faith in order to see the distinction between Christian and non-Christian forms of faith. The average Christian should be able to understand that because two faiths apply the same name to God, they do not necessarily worship the same God. Such an understanding must be tempered by a humility that is willing to learn from those who call themselves non-Christian and who sometimes possess a deeper knowledge of human sufferings, aspirations, and hopes. An intelligent grasp of world religions may be helpful for a better understanding of the distinctiveness of the Christian faith. If Christians take the claims of Christianity seriously, they will discover the " scandal of particularity," the ground of Christianity's amazing and even shocking inclusiveness. Therefore our proper concern must be with the truth of the Christian faith. Adults must make up their minds and decide where they stand in their relation to the claims made by Christianity.

Training Leaders

Fred Denbeaux, in his book *Understanding the Bible*, calls the church a " community of scholars " or a " small university." If we take this seriously, then one of the significant areas in Christian adult education in the church is preparing or training leaders for teaching. The problem of teachers is a serious one, and we have to face it with utmost seriousness. Some are of the opinion that as long as adults have some idea of how to handle a question (not necessarily answering it or clarifying it), as long as they know how to keep order and have some experience in " handling " children and youth, they are good teachers. This is, as someone has said, nothing but " miseducation." Actually, our purpose should be to use a sustained effort to enlarge the company of those who have a working knowledge of the Christian faith, as well as skills and tools necessary for effective teaching.

In the wider sense, training means helping those who teach to have a deeper understanding of the meaning of the Christian faith. We firmly believe that it is sheer wishful thinking to expect children and youth to grow in the Christian faith if no continuing education is taking place among those who have the responsibility of teaching. In the author's presence a child was asked, " What did you learn in Sunday school today? " She replied, " Same as last Sunday." We should not expect our children to increase their knowledge if no corresponding growth of equal importance is taking place among the teachers. How often training leaders has meant teaching teachers the answers they should impart to children and youth! Unless our teachers and leaders understand and experience these meanings for themselves, they are not able to give answers and interpret meanings. Once when a teacher told a child she had to learn from the minister how to answer his question, the child said: " Don't tell me what the minister says. Tell me what you know."

Teachers should also have a working knowledge of how children, youth, and adults learn and grow. They must have an understanding of their problems, anxieties, and aspirations. Although separate classes are desirable for teachers, it is the opinion of the author that teachers should be encouraged to participate in study groups with other adults for a confrontation with each other. How can adults be encouraged to teach unless they hear the testimony of those who teach not because they have to but because they want to; not because they have a great deal of information but because they are humble enough to learn and be tutored by the Holy Spirit; not because it is easy but because teaching means intellectual struggle as well as spiritual wrestling with ideas that matter most.

In the narrow sense, training means to put the emphasis on helping teachers to learn or to improve certain skills and procedures. It also means to equip them with better understanding of their students and of the subject matter; hence the importance of skill shops, leadership schools, and tutoring sessions by the minister or director of religious education. Leadership training may also develop group leadership and effective member participation.

Thus we need teachers who can learn to discern meanings and how to impart them, who are able to develop a process of critical thinking, and who are willing to continue growing in faith and knowledge. Our purpose is to have a corps of sensitive teachers with strong conviction, who are willing to devote energy and time to ideas that are matters of life and death, who are outgoing and warm in their relationships, and who teach, share, and witness — all " under God."

The question is, Is it possible to make such a vision a reality? The answer is, It is better to aim at such a possibility than to bemoan the fact that " our church does not have people of this caliber " or to cry, " How can we find these people? " It has been the experience of the author that such an idea is a real possibility, and that we can have such people on the waiting list to teach. When the church makes the teaching task seem easy and comforts people by assuring them: " Here is the book you will teach. The lessons are all planned and don't take too long to prepare," our teaching is doomed to failure. Such an expectation can be realized when the recruiting of teachers is a continuous searching process rather than an appeal from the pulpit the Sunday before the church school begins. And finally, this can be a reality when adults are *challenged* with the difficulty and the importance of the task of teaching. In every congregation there are persons with resources of intellectual interests and various experiences of group leadership. They should be sought, encouraged, challenged, and promised help in teaching.

What has been said so far leads us to consider a program for adult education in a local church. We have to keep in mind that the pattern varies in different locales. Every congregation that has enough people ought to offer a variety of courses of short duration of eight to twelve weeks. A stated length of time attracts new people who have different needs and capacities. It introduces them into new groups and thus allows them to choose the courses they want. Such a procedure prevents those groups which continue indefinitely from becoming ingrown and developing into cliques. Here we are in agreement with Fry, who refers to " contract groups " that specify the time when the study will terminate.

Introductory courses in the Bible and the basic Christian beliefs should be considered as a must in any program of adult education. They may serve as a starting point for the beginners and lead into more advanced and specialized courses. Each year there would be new courses, varied sufficiently so that adults could take up some new aspect of the faith for continuity and depth of study.

How to start study groups and how to multiply them is an important question that confronts most churches. Ministers and Christian educators are usually discouraged by the fact that a relatively small percentage of the congregation participates in any formal adult study group. This indeed is a discouraging and sobering fact. However, we are also aware of the fact that the adult constituency has never been more ready to want to learn; therefore, instead of complaining that laymen are religious illiterates, indifferent, complacent, we should recognize the interest of the few, encourage it and direct it. This is the chance that we ought not to miss — to take seriously the potential and the creative opportunity of working with small numbers of interested and committed people.

The experience of the author has been that of starting with groups as few as two and as many as twenty or more. Some were motivated by a personal crisis, some by crises in the life of the church — the sudden tragic death of a family on Christmas Eve; an accident to a high school girl, who was left paralyzed, dumb, deaf, and blind for the rest of her life. Some responded to an invitation by the minister or director of Christian education, and others were motivated by, " I want to know more about Christianity." A good starting point is with parents who are concerned with the religious growth of their children and are worried about their own spiritual maturity.

In short, any rigidly organized or institutionalized program of Christian adult education such as described in *The Institutional Nature of Adult Christian Education,* by Bruce Reinhart, is not only useless but deadly. On the other hand, free and voluntary participation should be encouraged, for this is certainly an opportunity for the church and a challenge for adventurous types of adult education.

After having said all this, let us not forget the fact that adult education is already taking place in sermons, Scriptures, sacraments, hymns, prayers, architecture, art. Further, each committee and each board of the church is and should be involved in some kind of adult education. How to make these experiences into learning opportunities is the responsibility of the minister and the director of Christian education.

METHODS OF STUDY

After such foundations are established, what is to be said concerning the method of Christian education for adults?

All planning for adults should take seriously the problem of teaching methods. What is the most effective means of communicating the Christian faith to adults, of conveying or sharing ideas? How can we decide whether or not any method is appropriate to Christian education? How can we measure their effectiveness? What are the relative values of the different methods of teaching? These are important questions if one cares for results.

Christian educators would agree that in addition to our understanding of the Christian doctrine of man, we should look at disciplines outside the church for ways of understanding human development and interpersonal relationship, for educational theory and practice, and for various methods and skills of communication, and we should learn how to adapt these facts to the specific problems of Christian education. But the problem has been that too many methods are known to be absolute and nonproductive. We have already quoted Bergevin, who points out that one of the problems that plague adult Christian education is the use of inappropriate and inadequate secular methodology.

Thus, methodology is intimately and inseparably connected with one's interpretation of the Christian faith, and it is functionally related to the purpose of Christian education. If our purpose is to lead persons into fuller realization of their potentialities as human creatures made in the image of God, then our teaching procedures will be effective when they help adults to come to an understanding of what they were created to be. This means that our methods should be kept open and varied so that individuals can freely explore the meaning of the Christian faith for themselves and be able to make their own decisions.

It is not the purpose of this discussion to offer a detailed account of teaching methods or techniques. The idea known as " The Indiana Plan for Adult Education," expanded in the book *Design for Adult Education in the Church*, by Bergevin and McKinley (The Seabury Press, Inc., 1958), is a very valuable source. It attempts to help educators learn how to practice as well as acquire the needed background for teaching methods. Our purpose in the following pages is to help the reader to recognize the values of some teaching methods that are in harmony with our purpose, keeping also in mind that no method, as such, can be truly consistent with the purpose of Christian adult education.

It is usually recognized that different methods of teaching make use of many more of the potential forces in the group than are brought to bear in the usual situation. Various procedures, such as the lecture, discussion, panel, symposium, book report, sociodrama, or a meaningful and intelligent combination of these methods, could be quite helpful. The fact is that we cannot afford rigidly controlled methods. Rather, the choice of educational methods should be determined by the nature of the group — the experiences and needs of the participants, the quality of leadership resources, and the nature of subject matter. It is well to quote an educator who believes that adults can learn by almost any method once they wake up from their dogmatic slumbers. Thus, when we establish certain procedures or techniques as being "correct," we immediately deny the individual differences of groups. We forget that every group has its own dynamics, its own pattern of forces and structure. Sometimes, of course, certain of these forces seem at a very minimum, but their potentiality exists in any group situation. Furthermore, we overlook the need to understand the specific condition of the group with which we are working at that particular time.

Within recent years, there has been a great emphasis upon group dynamics, and there are those who believe that this method in itself is the desired end and can solve most of our teaching problems. The subject of group dynamics has received critical treatment at the hands of many churchmen as well as of persons like William H. Whyte, Jr., the author of *The Organization Man,* who has prejudiced the popular understanding. Whatever the case, we call the reader's attention to the origin and the development of this branch of social psychology and to the writings of Kurt Lewin, the founder of group process, at the time when sociologists were concerned with reducing tension and bringing about adjustment. In this discussion we want to indicate that the question whether to use group dynamics or not has lost its impetus. The main issue is how seriously we want to take the dynamics of the group. To put the matter more clearly, How much attention do we wish to pay to the social and psychological forces of the nature of the group and the factors operating therein?

Group Discussion

There are different kinds of groups: a small group, composed of twelve to twenty persons — small enough for personal interaction; and a larger group, which eventually may be broken into small discussion groups for short periods of time.

Some of these groups are loosely structured, and others offer a more formal teaching situation. Once a group was started under a very permissive method. It did not take long for the leader to discover a sense of inadequacy on the part of the members. This method aroused anxiety and blocked the thinking of the members of the class. As a result, the group became convinced that this was a waste of time and asked the leader to assume a more active role. Another time a free discussion method reduced the subject matter to idly gossiping about God. Once a lecture method encouraged blank looks, nodding heads, and even a few snoozes! How often we allow adults to distort the Christian message through chitchat conversations and thus deepen the ignorance that is already there!

Now we ask the question of how we can judge the value of group discussion method in the light of our purpose. In other words, if our purpose is to help adults to come to an understanding of their destiny as a result of encounter with God in Jesus Christ, and if learning is growth in understanding this relationship, does group discussion have any value?

At this point we do not intend to give a detailed account of the meaning and value of group discussion; books and articles have been published in this field that are familiar to most of our readers. Rather, our purpose is to discuss very briefly how a group discussion can meet some of the problems we have raised in the previous chapters.

What is a discussion? A good discussion is a serious, disciplined, and conscious exploration of ideas that evokes critical thinking and enables the members of the class to ask questions, face crucial problems, share ideas, and make decisions. In other words, this is a social interaction which is a give-and-take of ideas and opinions by the members of the group as they encounter one another. We need not theologize or " proof-text " to defend the value of group discussion. The church through the ages has always recognized the principles of group activities and developed the idea of social interaction within its community. What is important for us to understand is the interaction that takes place among the members of a group, the dynamics of that interaction, and whether or not the results of this interaction are in accord with the purpose of Christian adult education.

First, each person in the group tends to respond to different persons in different situations. In our discussions we come across persons with different temperaments and emotional makeup. For instance, in Chapter II, we mentioned the man who thinks so much about himself that he can never be wrong. He gets much satisfaction from the fact that his ideals or beliefs are far beyond those in the group. Often he holds on to his single view so tightly that he finds it difficult to tolerate another's view, especially when it differs sharply from his own. The aggressive self attacks others.

He shows his disgust and antagonism when someone expresses an opinion. He protects himself by undermining the positions of others and belittling their opinions, and does not want to learn.

Here is an outgoing person who is able to relate readily to others. He not only accepts the members of the group but is able to draw others into discussion. He is willing to give as well as to receive and thus enter into a dialogue with others. The retiring self, on the other hand, withdraws when he encounters other selves. The passive, dependent self permits others to think and do things for him. The person who craves affection seeks attention in various ways. He is overtalkative; he agrees with others readily and shows approval easily.

In a discussion where human interaction takes place, each person affects the other and causes some kind of reaction that results in a give-and-take. In the following paragraphs we are interested in some of the significant aspects of the dynamics of this interaction.

As we have repeatedly pointed out, many adults have developed subtle habits of nonreflective thinking and have rigid " mental sets " that have made them less flexible in developing critical faculties. They need to experience the social interaction in which divergent viewpoints are subjected to critical inquiry and unreflective generalizations are brought into scrutiny. In such a discussion, at its best, there is the creative impulse of minds meeting one another. As a person defends his own position and learns to listen to others, he gets involved in a process of reflective thinking. Some of his cherished misconceptions of years are corrected, and others are discarded and replaced by more meaningful ones. As the members of the group talk they respond to one another by agreeing or differing, by clarifying or modifying their ideas. What is actually happening is that an inward intellectual exercise is taking place. Each opinion, idea, or interpretation that is uttered is a response to what was said previously. This is a creative process in which real thinking is taking place and new aspects of truth continue to emerge.

We have pointed out that many laymen do not participate freely in a discussion and would rather sit and listen. Some are afraid to reveal their lack of knowledge about religious matters; others are fearful of being misunderstood and are terrified by open disagreement. Still others suffer from a feeling of inadequacy. " I can't express my ideas well," or " I'm afraid to say it out loud." In a discussion it is possible to help adults overcome fear and suspicion and develop freedom of expression.

A permissive atmosphere that makes maximum freedom of expression possible encourages adults to allow their doubts, confusions, misconceptions, and rebellions to come out into the open instead of keeping them hidden behind various forms of rationalizatons or driving them away from awareness altogether. As we have seen, people often commit their minds to certain articles of faith in order to escape their own inner uncertainties and in so doing find spiritual relief and satisfaction. In order to pass from defensive rationalization to secure faith they need to face honestly and deeply what they have accepted consciously or unconsciously to be Christian. In a situation of give-and-take, the predicament of the skeptic, as well as that of the believer who takes it all too simply or finds religion a support to his complacency, may be explored and explained. They may be challenged to examine why they believe what they believe and to find out whether their convictions can stand the test of time and everyday experience. In such a situation, some are challenged to cast aside every false pretense; others are helped not to pretend to believe what they do not. Questions may be asked in such a way as to bring to the surface what seems to lie dimly in the depth. Even a partial answer may illumine the character of the faith a person holds.

Another significant aspect of the dynamics of interaction is that such a situation allows for two-way communication that leads into deepening fellowship with one another in the life of faith. On the deeper level this is an " I-Thou " relationship — a relationship of acceptance, when the self is released to affirm the other self. As the dialogue deepens, the members assist each other to perceive new meanings, to arrive at new insights. Such an understanding, which is not the result of new information or theory to which one has given intellectual assent, may lead to a change of position.

Such an interaction may be destructive when the changes it produces in persons are such as to weaken the will, harden the conscience, intensify feelings of hostility, increase dependence on others, confirm the existing prejudices, and damage the morale. On the other hand, if such an interaction leads the adults into fuller realization of who they are and what they were created for, then the method of group discussion may be in accord with our purpose of Christian adult education. We believe that as members of the class struggle with problems of faith, they will realize that they are confronted by the living God who stands over against whatever is destructive and seeks to impart himself in judgment and redemption and to lead them into deeper responsiveness to himself and to one another. When this knowledge becomes the basis of our understanding of ourselves, the deep sources of doubt, pride, and rebellion, dissolve in that inexplicable change of mind called repentance.

We shall conclude this section by asserting that in speaking so favorably about group discussion we do not ignore the lecture method, which, if properly used, is important and valuable. Most educators, however, agree that this method has two disadvantages for two main reasons. First, it is teaching by telling. In other words, it is telling people what they should know instead of guiding their thinking. Besides, without an expression of thought on the part of adults, the lecturer cannot tell what thoughts the people are harboring and what they need for growth. Secondly, listen-

ing develops the habit of depending on someone to tell what
the learners ought to know instead of helping them to assume the responsibility of thinking and deciding for themselves.

The Role of the Leader

Some very informal groups are loosely structured and
have no designated leaders. Sometimes certain committees,
planning groups, and teachers' meetings have rotating leadership. Some study groups select a particular book or pamph-
let and hold a number of meetings discussing it. John Fry
recommends " contract groups." A contract group has a
teacher, but the teacher is a book or a series of books.

We cannot afford to dismiss the variety of group leadership as means to effective guidance, but we should also be
critical of the group-directed as well as the leader-directed
teaching-learning situation. For instance, group-directed
Christian adult education is often evaluated in terms of how
many books laymen have read or how many sessions they
have attended. Sometimes a discussion may be said to have
met the emotional needs of the participants, which may
have a place in therapy, but it cannot be substituted for
what we have in mind as a purpose for Christian education.
On the other hand, some groups are dominated by the leader.
The leaders get carried away with their own pet ideas and
prejudices and aim at changing people's ideas from one theological point of view to another, or converting the adults to
their own newly acquired or " learned " position, thus leav-
ing people confused and anxious.

Our explanation of the discussion method in the previous
pages indicates that neither the group-centered nor the
leader-centered emphasis is the dominant factor. For our
purpose is not to reduce tension and bring about adjustment
by molding opinions, nor is it to let one person, presumably
the leader, dominate the discussion. The purpose is that all
shall be seekers after truth. Both the leader and the mem-

bers of the group would be working together in providing a setting for freedom of expression and acceptance. Both would be working toward a deeper understanding of God's activity in the human situation. However, this does not mean that the leader does not have a definite role. As a matter of fact, it is the author's conviction that adult education requires trained leadership in content, methodology, and conviction. The leader is not just a resource person to be dismissed when the group decides his role as that of information giver is ended. The leader is not the one who opens windows and arranges chairs. The powers of leadership have been entrusted to him to employ his particular skills and gifts in providing the necessary guidance to the group. Specifically, the leader should see that his role is to initiate, clarify, stimulate, guide, and give information. He is able to bring about the group interaction necessary for thinking, sharing, and making decisions. He encourages the members of the group to raise their own questions and to seek their own answers. And in doing that he realizes that he too asks his own questions and seeks his own answers. It is believed that the genius of group discussion is to " evoke the unexpected," and so the leader requires a broad range of explanations in order to be able to face new and unexpected situations.

We would like to call the reader's attention to *A Theology of the Laity,* by Hendrik Kraemer. This little volume presents a new appreciation of the unique role of every Christian as a leader and a learner in the community of faith, and as one called to lead as well as learn and be obedient to the promptings of the Holy Spirit.

The Problem of Language

The question of language is a primary issue in communicating the Christian faith, and thus of utmost importance in the educational process.

It should be remembered that language is historical and particular, never static and general. All words, in fact, have history, and some of them unusual adventures. For instance, one would hardly see the connection between the attic of his house and the Attic architectural glory of ancient Greece. Furthermore, meanings subtly change until they almost reverse their original meaning, i.e., " security " and "comfort." Thus, language has many possible meanings, and it is necessary to know the various uses and the various implications of each use.

The content of the words or phrases of Christian language is of great potency and has the power to influence human thought and behavior. Theological and Biblical language is capable not only of eliciting reactions to emotionally conditioned phrases and words but also of stirring human motivations. Certain words evoke anger and cause a short circuit in discussions. Often there is resistance among adults occasioned by language norms that attempt to replace words grown dear by habitual association. Many laymen have become callous to warmed-over stereotypes and to Biblical terms that have turned into pious clichés, such as " sin," " salvation," " holy," " repentance." Words like: " Christ-centered," " child-centered," " church-centered," convey little or no meaning to laymen even when they are explained. Certain words, such as " existential," " confrontation," " fellowship," are losing their value in the frequency of their occurrence.

Easy generalizations of the meaning of certain important words are in danger of becoming masks for ignorance. It is necessary, therefore, that adults before they speak think painfully about the meaning and limits of their language. On one occasion the author did what D. T. Niles tried in a seminary class. The conversation went like this: " You have been in this class for two months. Think of me as a person with average intelligence. I have never been to church. I have never read the Bible. The family from which I come is also unbelieving. I never finished high school. I work in a factory on an assembly line."

The first thing the members of the class did was to extend an invitation to go to church. When asked why, they said, " In order to hear God's Word." To which I responded: " I don't know what you are talking about. I have never heard the Word of God before! " For fifteen minutes the members of the class talked, using words like " sin," " grace," " salvation," while I kept on saying: " I don't understand. Please use words that I can understand." Finally the class agreed that " there just ain't such a human being."

These considerations, obvious enough in themselves, remind us that the nature and significance of language is a serious matter; therefore, Christian educators need to become sensitive to the problem of effective verbal communication. There should be a genuine concern for proper meaning and use of terms lest language degenerate into a vague and complicated kind of Scrabble game. What we are really concerned with is the task of interpretation. Our responsibility is to insist upon clarity and rigor of language in order to convey meanings with a minimum loss of mutual understanding. It is our duty to be the translators of the Christian faith into the language, the idiom, and the minds of adults and youth. What we say must be intelligible, otherwise no meaning is conveyed and speech is not heard.

This is not to say that the old vocabulary must be discarded. As a matter of fact, the language of the Christian faith is historical as well as existential and contemporary. Laymen should become acquainted with the language of the faith they profess, which in another discipline would be a basic requirement. The old language embodies eternal truths that are to be understood and heeded. But we also want to emphasize that new meanings should arise and develop. New impetus should be given to ancient meanings of myth, symbol, metaphor, and analogy. Adults should realize that truth is never really simple; therefore, it is necessary when dealing with profound matters and describing the deeper changes in the self to speak in symbols, myths, poetry, stories, rather than in exact propositions. The question of how and why certain things are said and what is actually meant by them is important. We may substitute " courage to be " for " justification by faith," " new being " for " salvation," or we may use " meeting " instead of " confrontation," " personal " for " existential." Crude metaphors such as " throwness " or " the isness of it all " may break through the protective barricades of specialized jargon, and intrigue people for a while. But we should also remember that if the language of the Bible is remote for men today, this new language is even more remote. To emulate secular ideas by " inventing " new terminology that is Christianly unrecognizable is to defeat our purpose. It would certainly seem far easier to clarify meaning to laymen by explaining the language of the Bible than by replacing it by a more difficult way of speaking. Even the new terms by which we explain are subject to the ambiguity of our personal experience and cultural settings. Further, after the novelty wears off, we are still left confronted with great symbolic and mythical truths: " In the beginning God created the heavens and the earth," " And the Word became flesh," " God was in Christ," " Before Abraham was, I am," which must be understood and sharpened in the whole depth and breadth of their meaning. These statements enshrine the deepest mystery of the Christian faith because they refer to something beyond human existence. They need to be interpreted and made intelligible in such a way as to allow room for differences of individual interpretations and thought forms.

By no means do we wish to imply that a concern for language should become a fetish. It is necessary, however, to learn from linguistic analysis and modern analytical philosophy, and even be acquainted with the vocabulary of other disciplines, especially that of natural sciences. They all help us to become aware of certain perplexing issues and enable us to analyze the variety of the church's languages.

In summary, we believe that our language is a conviction as well as an experience. For Willem Zuurdeeg, convictional language is not a tool to be used and discarded. Rather, it is the person who speaks, and the man who speaks is totally involved in his convictions, and he refers to something that is real for him.[30] The language we use is expressive of our own situation in regard to ourselves, to others, and to the world. We cannot escape the fact that people force us to a radical and patient expression of our own faith and make us realize that we cannot live by a truth that we are unable and unwilling to express.

It is true that our explanations are often clumsy and tedious and stifle the spontaneity of our laymen. Nevertheless, our words stand in need of witnessing expression, and the force of our statements depends upon the depth of the conviction they express. Our language can be understood, given resourcefulness, humility, patience, and the power of the Holy Spirit. After all, what is offered in teaching is not merely a set of facts to be believed, ready-made answers to be accepted, or spelled-out applications of the Christian truth to be obeyed. Teaching may mean all these and more. Actually, Christian education is education into experience, and essentially what is offered is a relationship to be experienced. Christian language is relational in character. Its doctrine of God means redemption, reconciliation, grace; its doctrine of man means sin, repentance, forgiveness. The question, How does God reconcile us to himself? must be answered out of the experience that he does. Thus, we should aim at being understood for what we believe and what we experience and not for some travesty of it.

In summary, we believe that language can facilitate understanding as well as become a barrier to communicating the faith. But let us also assert that the real problem of communication is not confined to language alone, but implies the communication of the Christian life of faith. Adults cannot remain educated, well-informed, and even repented Christians. They should be able to act out of their faith as they live in the world and communicate their faith through the manifestation of " the fruit of the Spirit . . . love, joy, peace, . . . self-control " (Gal. 5:22-23), which have been given to the believers as the gifts of God's grace in Jesus Christ so that they may be ambassadors for Christ as the messengers of reconciliation (II Cor. 5:19-20).

EPILOGUE

An attempt to conclude our foregoing discussion must begin by asking once more where our laymen are and what the church intends for them.

The general picture given by most educators is that adults are not believing or humble, that they willfully resist ideas and refuse to learn; that they are indifferent, disinterested, and lack normal curiosity; that they are full of prejudices, fanaticism, naïve illusions, superstitions. John Fry says, " The typical student, as a typical human being, according to the Bible, is antigospel, anti-Jesus Christ, and anti-God; pro-past, pro-world, pro-lies, and pro-death." [31]

To a certain extent our previous discussion confirms the fact that these descriptions are variously true, and yet with the language of the officers in *Hamlet*:

> Sit down a while
> And let us once again assail your ears,
> That are so fortified against our story.

In the first place, the modern adult is none other than the Biblical man, created in God's image, yet alienated from him by his egocentricity and pride. However, he is not left to self-destruction but called back to communion with God through Jesus Christ. Nonetheless, man finds the real barrier to faith the surrender of his self-sufficiency and the refusal to live in dependence on and in communion with God.

Further, the modern man is the adult of the twentieth-century Christianity of the Western world, and his problems are the problems of man in the perplexing world of technology and science, which seek to depersonalize and to abstract human problems and thus to remove responsibility and guilt from the stage of human history.

After saying all this, let us hasten to add that our judgment of adults should be tempered by compassion to believe in the infinite significance of the person as the beloved of God, and by courage to believe in God's promise of the redemption of man. To have a deep concern for people is the central concern of the church itself. For the core of the Christian message is simply and solely the story of God's concern for man. For man's sake, God became man in order to lay hold of him and draw him to himself.

Therefore, the more passionately we are concerned with interpreting the Christian faith, the more earnestly we must strive with people; the more seriously we take the gospel message, the more concerned we must be with man. We must realize that indications of indifference, unawareness, and antagonism are attempts to cover up the real yearning of people for reconciliation with God and man.

Christian education of adults today faces a unique opportunity to enlist its energies in the effort to meet the challenge of the emerging church. Therefore, every difficulty should be made an opportunity for adventurous types of Christian adult education, and every perplexity must be made the ground of patient exploration.

NOTES

1. *Christianity and Crisis*, Vol. XXII, No. 10 (June 11, 1962).
2. Fred J. Denbeaux, *The Art of Christian Doubt* (Association Press, 1960), p. 68.
3. Paul Tillich, *Systematic Theology*, Vol. 1 (The University of Chicago Press, 1950), p. 8.
4. William Temple, *Nature, Man and God* (The Macmillan Company, 1935), p. 322.
5. Hugh Martin, *Puritanism and Richard Baxter* (SCM Press Ltd., London, 1954), p. 129.
6. Søren Kierkegaard, *Attack Upon Christendom* (Beacon Press, Inc., 1956).
7. See Franklin Le Van Baumer, *Religion and the Rise of Scepticism* (Harcourt, Brace & World, Inc., 1960).
8. Emil Brunner, *Revelation and Reason* (The Westminster Press, 1946), p. 208.
9. Paul Tillich, *The Dynamics of Faith* (Harper & Row, Publishers, Inc., 1957), p. 20.
10. *Ibid.*, p. 22.
11. Gustaf Aulén, *The Faith of the Christian Church*, tr. by Eric H. Wahlstrom and G. Everett Arden (Muhlenburg Press, 1948), p. 325.
12. Lewis J. Sherrill, *The Gift of Power* (The Macmillan Company, 1959), p. 82.
13. John R. Fry, *A Hard Look at Adult Christian Education* (The Westminster Press, 1961), p. 107.
14. *Ibid.*, pp. 104–106.
15. Philip H. Phenix, *Education and the Common Good: A*

Moral Philosophy of the Curriculum (Harper & Row, Publishers, Inc., 1961), p. 242.

16. Alan Richardson, ed., *A Theological Word Book of the Bible* (The Macmillan Company, 1951), pp. 191 ff.

17. Emil Brunner, *The Christian Doctrine of Creation and Redemption* (The Westminster Press, 1952), p. 257.

18. John Calvin, *Calvin: Commentaries,* tr. and ed. by Joseph Haroutunian in collaboration with Louise Pettibone Smith (The Library of Christian Classics, The Westminster Press, 1958), p. 228.

19. Richardson, *op. cit.,* p. 122.

20. Rudolf Bultmann, *Primitive Christianity and Its Contemporary Setting* (Living Age Books, Meridian Books, Inc., 1956), p. 181.

21. Reinhold Niebuhr, *Beyond Tragedy* (Charles Scribner's Sons, 1937), pp. 149–150.

22. Fry, *op. cit.,* p. 126.

23. Robert McAfee Brown, *The Spirit of Protestantism* (Oxford University Press, Inc., 1961), p. 122.

24. Brunner, *Revelation and Reason,* p. 217.

25. *Ibid.,* pp. 216–217.

26. *Evaluation and Christian Education* (National Council of the Churches of Christ in the U.S.A., 1959), pp. 26–27.

27. Brown, *op. cit.,* p. 123.

28. Temple, *op. cit.,* p. 30.

29. Lawrence C. Little, ed., *The Future Course of Christian Adult Education* (University of Pittsburgh Press, 1959), p. 127.

30. Willem F. Zuurdeeg, *An Analytical Philosophy of Religion* (Abingdon Press, 1958), p. 45.

31. Fry, *op. cit.,* p. 92.